The Architecture of Japan

The Architecture of Japan

BY ARTHUR DREXLER

THE MUSEUM OF MODERN ART, NEW YORK

Library of Congress Catalog Card Number: 55-5987

CONTENTS

PREFACE AND ACKNOWLEDGMENTS

This book is concerned with architecture in Japan from ancient times to the present. The first section is devoted to the environment and some of the religious beliefs which have influenced all Japanese art. The second section is concerned with general principles of structure and design peculiar to Japanese architecture, and the third section is devoted primarily to buildings considered masterpieces by the Japanese themselves. Gardens in Japan are a separate art form, but because they play a part in Japanese architecture so much greater than in our own they have been treated here with appropriate detail.

A supplement, beginning on page 262, is devoted to the Japanese Exhibition House built in the garden of the Museum of Modern Art and open to the public during the summers of 1954 and 1955.

Farm houses, castles, and folk architecture in general have been included only incidentally. However beautiful such buildings may be, they convey inadequately the power and subtlety of the art of architecture in Japan. The selection of buildings for detailed presentation has also been influenced to some extent by considerations of their relevance to contemporary Western architecture.

The relevance of Japan's architectural tradition to contemporary Western building is well known. Modern Western practice, with its general use of the steel skeleton frame, has developed effects known to Japanese architecture at least since the eighth century. Walls which do not support a roof but are instead hung like curtains on a structural framework are today a commonplace of Western building. Before 1900 Frank Lloyd Wright made fundamental to his work a Japanese respect for the beauty of natural materials, as well as the hovering, insistently horizontal roofs essential to the Japanese conception of a house. Open interiors and plain surfaces, as in the work of Mies van der Rohe and Le Corbusier, are other ideas characteristic of Japan which we have been developing in our own way.

Japanese culture has been altered by industrialization even more drastically than has the culture of the Western world. The ordinary problems of industrialization, compounded with conflicts between Eastern and Western cultural values, have been resolved in Japan largely by the conscious acceptance of two different and sometimes opposed ways of life, one traditionally Japanese, the other more or less Western. Although some architects never entirely abandoned the old principles of building, modern architecture in Japan has evolved, perhaps of necessity, primarily along Western lines. Only recently have their traditional values begun to attract the sympathetic study of Japan's younger architects.

The art of building will of course continue to develop, in Japan as in the West, as the expression of attitudes toward life in the twentieth century. A part of that life is the growing exchange of ideas between the East and the West. Japanese architecture conveys the attitudes and the aspirations of its country with a complexity surpassed only by its beauty.

I wish to thank the many people in Japan and the United States who assisted in the preparation of this book. Above all I am grateful to Ryuichi Hamaguchi for accompanying me on my travels in Japan, and to Junzo Yoshimura for his enlightening comments. The authorities of Ise Shrine, and Nagakage Okabe, Director of the National Museum of Modern Art in Tokyo, made it possible for me to see the innermost buildings of the Shinto Shrine at Ise Naiku, before the latest reconstructions were consecrated, and subsequently to publish here the first authorized photographs. Harumichi Kitawo has kindly permitted the use of drawings from his fifteen volume history of *Shoin-zukuri* architecture. I have also drawn from books on Japanese life and architecture by Jiro Harada, Sutemi Horiguchi, Tetsuro Yoshida, Shinze Koike, A. L. Sadler, Edward Conze, and Alexander C. Soper III. No student of Japan can fail to be grateful to Sir George Sansom; I have drawn especially from his *Japan, a Short Cultural History,* and *The Western World and Japan.* Alexander C. Soper III has very generously given his time to reading the text and making many valuable suggestions. Translations of Japanese texts were made by Yoshinobu Ashihara and Tamiko Niwa; Chisaburoh Yamada provided additional information. Philip Johnson assisted with editing the text, and I am grateful to Mildred Constantine for her assistance on all phases of the preparation of the book.

On behalf of the Museum I wish to thank most especially Mr. and Mrs. John D. Rockefeller 3rd. Their generous contribution and enthusiastic interest made possible the size and scope of both the book and the exhibition.

A.D.

1

Japanese creation myths describe the primeval chaos as an ocean of mud. From this darkness celestial deities sprang forth spontaneously, among them Izanagi and Izanami, the male who invites and the female who invites. At the command of the celestial deities they descended to produce the terrestrial world. First of all they gave birth to the Japanese archipelago, then to waters, winds, mountains, fields, food, fire, and mist. And then they gave birth to the rulers of the world.

The rulers of the world, the creation myths continue, are Amaterasu O-mi-Kami, the Heaven Illuminating Goddess whose domain is heaven and earth and whose home is the sun; Tsuki-yomi, who rules the moon and whose domain is night; and Takehaya Susanowo, the Valiant Swift Impetuous Hero, the God of Storms who lives in the ocean and rules the domain of hidden things. Control of the world soon passed to Susanowo and his sister, the Sun Goddess. Bright, beautiful, and meek, she constructed canals to irrigate the rice fields and she organized religious rites—especially those pertaining to purity.

But Susanowo longed for his mother, who was now the evil genius of death and darkness. In his rage he destroyed the canals his sister had made in the fields, and when finally he profaned her religious observances her exasperation was so great that she withdrew into a cave, taking with her the light of the world. Then eight million deities assembled at the doors of the cave, persuading her to come out by dancing and reciting charms. Her curiosity was aroused. She peeked out of the cave to watch the dancing, and immediately strong deities forced open its doors and pulled her out. Light and order were restored. The eight million deities gave such a shout of joy that heaven and earth trembled—as they still do, from time to time.

In fact the earth trembles in Japan about twelve times a year in seismic shudders sufficient to crack windows and make roofs collapse. According to contemporary accounts of creation, the Japanese archipelago is one of a series of submerged mountain arcs lying off the coast of Asia. Rising from the Manshu Deep to summits four and five thousand feet above sea level, it was formed by violent block faulting and volcanic activity. Of Japan's one hundred and ninety-two volcanos, fifty-two have been active within historic times, and the Japanese islands owe their abrupt jagged configuration to crustal foldings and upheavals so recent, as geologists measure time, that the land has not yet been eroded to smoothness. Physically, economically, and culturally the Japanese mainland is Honshu. North of it lies Hokkaido, with a landscape like that of Maine. Clustered at the

U.S.S.R.
MANCHURIA
SAKHALIN
NIKOLAEVSK
VLADIVOSTOK
PORT ARTHUR
PYONGYANG
SAPPORO
HOKKAIDO
SEOUL
Sea of Japan
KOREA
POHANG
PUSAN
HONSHU
Tsushima Strait
HIROSHIMA
KURE
KOBE
NARA
KYOTO
NAGOYA
YOKOHAMA
Inland Sea
SASEBO
FUKUOKA
OSAKA
SHIKOKU
ISE
YOKOSUKA
NAGASAKI
KYUSHU
Pacific Ocean

southwest tip of Honshu are Shikoku and Kyushu; between these three is the Inland Sea, dotted with hundreds of smaller islands of a beauty which makes them comparable to that fabled island in the Japan Sea—Sado—"where even the grass would prefer to grow." No farmer can be more than forty miles from the sea, but visually the character of the landscape is determined by mountains. Less than one-seventh of Japan is level, and an area of 20,000 square miles, equal to about half the state of Ohio, accommodates most of the population of 80,216,000. The greatest contrasts are up and down rather than north and south: farmers look up from rice paddies to snow fields and the tree line. Orchids and palms, cryptomeria, oak and maple, pine, plum and cherry trees congregate in a climate like that from Maine to Georgia, although the humidity is constantly higher. Hot and moist masses of air from the tropical Pacific begin to drift over the islands in June, bringing the gentle "Plum Blossom" rains and a stifling mist which makes the Japanese remove and store away the exterior walls of their houses. In winter there are cold dry winds from Siberia, against which farmers on the western shores protect their buildings by weighting the roofs with stones.

The remote ancestors of those farmers, in the uneasy time before history begins, most probably came from a central point on the Asiatic mainland, possibly in South China or Indo-China, from which they emigrated to the southern Pacific islands, Korea, and Japan. There is no archeological evidence to support the belief that much of the Japanese population has its origin in the southern islands, despite the predominance and the continuing reassertion of architectural forms peculiar to the tropical Pacific, as well as the strong Malay cast of feature and bodily structure of much of the present population. The earliest remains are of the Jōmon people, and they suggest a northern continental or Caucasian origin. The Jōmon people were also similar to the Ainu population which they eventually displaced. Named for a kind of pottery decorated with a rope or coil pattern, Jōmon culture was itself succeeded by a people whose artifacts resemble those found in Korean excavations. This second phase of Japanese culture is called Yayoi, after the place in southern Honshu where most of its remains have been unearthed. The Yayoi succession was aided by fresh waves of cultural influence transmitted from the continent through Korea. Both the Jōmon and the early Yayoi cultures were neolithic, but when it displaced or absorbed the Jōmon people in the southern and western parts of Japan the Yayoi culture was about to pass into a metal phase. China's age of bronze was extended to Japan by the Yayoi people, but

RICE FIELDS

With less than one-seventh of the land level, farmers must terrace the mountainsides for the cultivation of rice. Stone retaining walls are used when the terraces are small and close together, but usually the walls are of earth cut and smoothed with a trowel.

was so rapidly overtaken by the Chinese iron age that Japan can not be said to have had a true bronze culture.

"In that land," says the Nihon-shoki (the Chronicles of Japan compiled in A.D. 720), referring to the time when the founders of the nation contemplated descending to earth, "there were numerous deities which shone with a lustre . . . and evil deities which buzzed like flies. There were also trees and herbs which could speak." Men, animals, plants and rocks, all things animate and inanimate, had speech and were *kami;* whatever evoked a thrill of awe, mystery, or affection, whatever possessed superior merit, was in some sense miraculous and therefore sacred: *kami.* The feeling of communion with nature which inspired this response was so deeply rooted that its picture of what the West calls the world beyond, but in Japan was regarded as the world within the natural world, evolved without a rigidly conceptualized theogony. The attributes of individual deities remained to a large degree interchangeable. Worship of these deities was only given a name—Shinto, The Way of the Gods—to distinguish it in the eighth century from the newly imported teachings of Buddhism. In a universe neither friendly nor hostile to man, and in which divinity was manifested in all things, the earliest teachings of Shinto described the soul as consisting of two parts: the first, *Nigi-mitama,* is mild, refined, essentially happy, and associated with health and prosperity; the second, *Ara-mitama,* is rough. It is also adventurous, dashing, and sometimes even evil. Since the soul was associated with breathing, to die was the departure of breath. The soul was a substance. Precious, round, and glowing, it could sometimes be seen lingering in the darkness, a pale ball of fire. It might or it might not go away: it did become *kami,* and it was necessary to prepare for it the appropriate accommodations.

The practice of building large burial mounds for the ruling class seems to have been economically feasible by the third century A.D., but after numerous Imperial proscriptions limiting the size of the mounds according to rank, and then altogether forbidding the aristocracy to continue in what had become a ruinous extravagance, it appears finally to have been abandoned around A.D. 600. Many of these burial mounds survive in central Japan, greatly modified by time and the weather. The extraordinary sculptures they contained reveal the foundations of a style volition peculiarly Japanese, by which subsequent inundations of Indian, Chinese, and, to a lesser extent, Western culture have all been transformed.

Of the four types of burial mounds that can be distinguished, two occur frequently enough to be taken as characteristic. In plan the first of these types is round; the second is roughly squared in front and rounded in back. Although in most cases they are now covered with trees and shrubs, originally these artificial plateaus were closely paved with thousands of white cobblestones. From one to three moats further isolated them from the landscape, and probably accounts for their having been called Elysian Isles. The largest of the mounds was made for the Emperor Nintoku, who died in A.D. 425. Ninety feet high and 1620 feet long, it has a rounded back 816 feet in diameter. Both sides of this mound have eroded, so that in plan it now presents a figure somewhat like a keyhole. The burial chamber of Nintoku's tomb was proportioned like a corridor 8 feet wide and 20 feet long, the walls and ceiling being built of great stone slabs. The tomb was surrounded by three moats, and both the mound and the area around the moats were fenced with stakes made of clay, called *haniwa*—literally circles of clay. These cylinders were placed close together and half buried in the ground, presumably to keep the mounds from being washed away by the rain. Eventually they acquired a symbolic content and were made not as unadorned cylinders but as men and women, warriors in battle dress, children, and animals. An agreeable legend, but probably an apocryphal one, relates that the slaves of Prince Yamato Hiko, on being buried alive with their deceased master, moaned and cried so movingly that the Emperor Suinin asked a court official if it were not possible, henceforth, to substitute symbolic statues of clay for living sacrifices. Emperor Nintoku's tomb, some two hundred and fifty years later, was arrayed with 11,280 cylinders deployed in three "man fences." Forty-eight hundred *haniwa* were outside the moat and 6480 were on the mound itself.

In contrast to the art forms of other cultures in a comparable stage of development, the esthetic characteristics of the *haniwa* figures seem motivated less by fear than by the Yayoi craftsmen's ineluctable urge to render more elegant the world of their experience. Brutality and the grotesque gave way, we may suppose, before a world whose population of deities represented indifferent trees, rocks and fireflies at least as copiously as storms, disasters, and unnatural evils. Many of the *haniwa* sculptures look as though they were made by rolling a sheet of clay into a cylinder and then closing it at the top. The force of the design is sustained chiefly by the taut linear quality of rounded openings cut sharply into the sides, to indicate eyes, nose, and mouth, and the preoccupation with line is echoed in contours which seem drawn rather than modeled. Suave and often witty, the *haniwa* images are fashioned with a repressed energy that

TOMB OF EMPEROR NINTOKU

Begun c. A.D. 425, near what is now called Osaka. Occupying 80 acres, Nintoku's tomb is an artificial mountain surrounded by three moats. Indentations at both sides of the mound are attributed to erosion.

Head of a girl. Nara, c. A.D. 300

HANIWA SCULPTURE

Right: Two dancers. Saitama Prefecture, c. A.D. 200. The difference in height distinguishes the man from the woman; the man is 17 inches high, but when placed in the ground only the upper part of the figure is visible.

Unlike China's Ming ch'i statues, which were representations of animals and men placed in tombs for eternal service to the deceased, *haniwa* images are often in full ceremonial dress and seem designed primarily to commemorate high rank.

TATEANA DWELLING
The oval pit was protected by a cone-shaped roof covered with bark or grass.

takes them, sometimes, to the edge of caricature. But they are not so much portraits of people as of attitudes and gestures.

Besides the *haniwa* figures, tools, and ornaments, the sepulchral mounds have yielded many clay models of dwellings and shrines, and there survive pictorial records engraved on clay tablets, the backs of mirrors, and in one case on a bronze bell, of building types thought to be among the earliest in Japan. There also remain a few actual sites pressed into the ground like footprints, where marks of posts, hearths, and entrances describe in vague and fading relief the techniques of building in a most ancient time.

The first dwellings were natural caves; then, near springs, cave dwellings were excavated in soft ground at the side of a hill. But the proper record of architecture begins with what remains in eastern Japan of the shallow pit dwellings now called *Tateana.* Conjectural reconstructions of these dwellings suggest that they coincided with, or even preceded, a simple gable roof resting on the ground, called *Tenchi-gongen.* And with them all in a realm of speculation are dwellings of a somewhat later period supposed to have been built on posts over water; though similar buildings can be found throughout the south Pacific, there is no evidence of their having been used widely, if at all, in Japan.

Tateana sites were roughly rectangular in plan, but with well-rounded corners transforming the rectangle into a crude oval about 17 feet long. The earth floor was from 2 to 3 feet below ground level, the sides of the pit forming a low vertical wall. In the middle of the floor an open hearth was either excavated or marked off by small stones. Inside the pit four posts were planted directly in the ground; four beams were laid across them. The arrangement of the posts coincides with the ground plans of huts built at a much later time for smelting iron sand, in southwestern Japan, and since these huts probably evolved from the earlier *Tateana* pit dwellings they provide some indication of how the roof was constructed. Rafters, springing from the ground outside the pit, rested on the beams and projected several feet above them. Single rafters centered on the narrow ends of the rectangular superstructure changed the perimeter of the roof, at ground level, into a circle rather like the base of a cone-shaped tent. Covered with bark, leaves, or grass, this roughly textured lid was given an additional sculptural quality by the ridge pole, which was made to extend well beyond the points at which the rafters supported it, thus forming a triangular peak on two sides of the roof. In time there developed some heroically massive versions of such roof formations. The triangular openings served for ventilation, but apart from its practical origin this ancient combination of shapes, found in Malay and the Celebes as well as in India, signifies to the Japanese today a warrior's helmet (the peaked upper section) and its neck guard (the circular base).

Dark and damp, the pit dwellings had at least the merit of maintaining a more equable year round temperature than did natural or artificial caves. In the next phase a floor at ground level counteracted dampness: of such houses, called *Hirachi,* the best preserved sites are those in which the floors were paved with stone; no example of the superstructure survives. And finally, when the floor was raised off the ground entirely, in the building type called *Takayuka,* Japanese architecture struck its characteristic and most enduring note. A drawing on a bronze bell of the first or second century A.D., found in Shikoku, shows a *Takayuka* structure with a gabled roof. Access to the raised floor is by means of a ladder placed at the narrow end of the gable. The ridge pole, no longer supported by the rafters as it was in the pit dwellings, is instead carried by two columns independent of the rest of the structure. A curious convention of perspective in the representation on the bronze bell, and in other drawings, makes the rafters seem to be flying away from the ridge pole rather than to be resting on it; what the drawing presumably intends to emphasize is the projection of the rafters above the ridge pole, where they cross each other and form twin decorative combs along the top of the roof. There is no particular structural justification for this detail, unless it be the provision of extra weight to keep the ridge pole balanced in place; but the decorative motif, called *chigi,* survives as a single pair of crossed rafters at each end of a building. It can be seen in shrines at Ise and elsewhere in Japan. Similar forms may be found in the southern Pacific islands and in southeastern Asia, where the crossed rafters sometimes are carved and painted; today there exist communities in India where, in the absence of wood, or perhaps simply out of preference for an exotic material, a kind of *chigi* are carefully cut from sheets of corrugated tin.

The early *Takayuka* dwellings were single cells of space. Isolated column supports for the roof were placed at each corner of this empty cube, and were structurally independent of the walls which completed the enclosure. The simplest way to amplify and extend this space was to place a column in the center and a column between each of the corner posts, implying a division of the single volume into four distinct cells. In farmhouses today the division of a square plan into four areas is often effected with four partitions which, radiating from the central post, reach halfway to the exterior

TAKAYUKA DWELLING

An engraving on a bronze plaque of the first or second century A.D. shows an elevated building called *Takayuka.* Two independent columns support the ridge pole; rafters rest against the ridge pole and project beyond it, forming decorations called *chigi.* Access is by a high steep ladder, suggesting that the building type may originally have been devised as a granary.

Haniwa representation of a dwelling or warehouse. Details of the wood framework are necessarily distorted in this clay model, but the cylindrical weights along the ridge and the heavy gable ends are rendered more accurately.

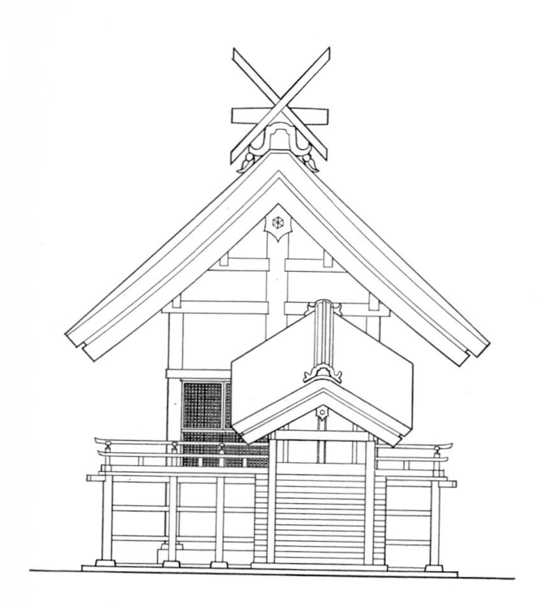

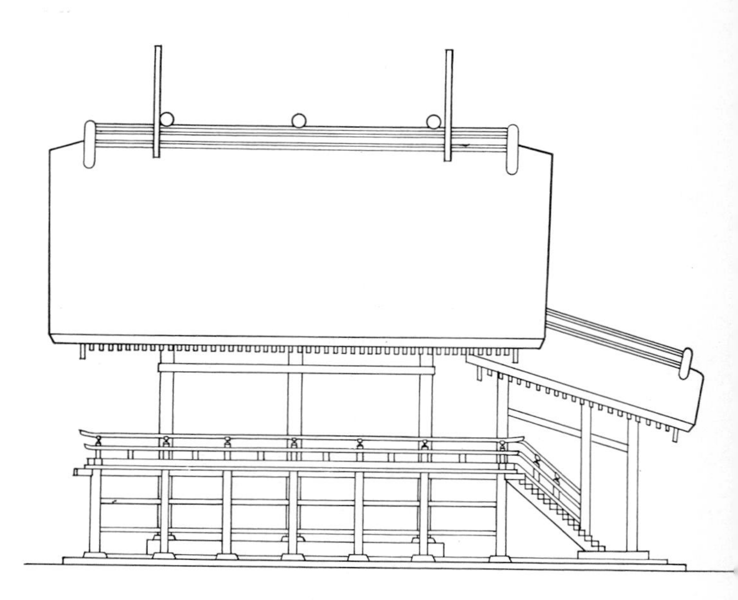

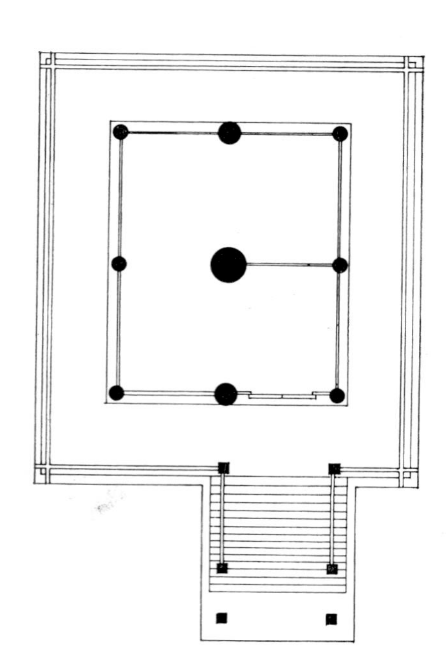

IZUMO SHRINE

The main building of Izumo Shrine is an elevated structure approximately 36 feet square without its verandas. First built prior to A.D. 550, the present reconstruction dates from 1744.

walls. It seems most probable that the original impetus for this spatial and structural elaboration—if there can be said to have been any single dominating impetus—was the desire to make some qualitative distinction, in shrines, between the space reserved for the deity as symbolized by an object associated with its powers, and the space reserved for priests. An example of one of the earliest usages of the four-celled plan is the shrine at Izumo; its arrangement reveals, in a state untutored by other cultural influences, the Japanese proclivity for asymmetrical composition. Entirely raised above ground level and surrounded by a veranda, the building is reached by a high steep stair whose off-center placement gives to the south facade its chief architectural interest. In this building the deity is enshrined in the northeast compartment, facing toward the west. Entrance to the building is through the southeast compartment. The only interior partition is that which screens the deity's cell from the adjoining entrance area: the two remaining units of space, on the west, are thrown together. The west elevation of the Izumo shrine faces the sea, presumably so that the deity, or the priest who sat at the deity's shrine, was able to gaze outward in placid contemplation.

Shrines are built to protect an object inhabited by a spirit. It is not the object itself which is the focus of worship, but the *kami* that has made the object its resting place. Features of the landscape like unusual stones and trees are in this sense *kami,* and were the original objects of worship; sometimes an entire forest, or a mountain like Fujiyama, was thus revered. But usually the holiness of an individual tree or stone was acknowledged by circling it with a wood fence. Artificial objects were also attractive to *kami:* the three sacred treasures of Japan are a jewel symbolizing knowledge; a sword, symbolizing authority; and a mirror that by the purity of its reflections symbolizes justice. Given by the gods to the remote ancestors of the Japanese, the mirror is perhaps the most important of the three great treasures, and the Emperor, as the chief intermediary between his people and the spirits, is custodian of the Sacred Mirror at Ise.

Ise, in southwest Honshu, is the most holy center of the Shinto religion, and the complex of buildings and fences which together constitute the shrine is perhaps the most impressive example of all Shinto architecture. Ise Naiku (the Inner Shrine, as distinguished from Ise Geku, a group of buildings three miles from it, erected in 478 for the grain goddess Toyouke-no-Okami) was founded late in the third century A.D. and is dedicated to the Sun Goddess Amaterasu O-mi-Kami. The site is in a forest of giant cryptomeria bordering the Isuzu River. What is properly called the shrine

ISE SHRINE

The prayer gate in the second fence, curtained with white silk, is the furthest point in the enclosure to which visitors may approach.

ISE SHRINE

Torii between the second and third fences. The structure in the background is a gate.

ISE SHRINE

The Shoden or main building, containing the sacred symbols of Shintoism; in the background is the west treasure house. The covered entrance is a detail added in the Meiji Era (1868-1912) to protect the steps.

comprises four rectangular buildings on a level clearing 55 yards wide by 127 yards long. Four fences, one within the other, completely enclose this site. The Shoden, or main building, and two treasure houses are located behind the innermost fence; a meeting hall for the priests lies between the second and third fences. The major axis of the site runs north-south, and it is from the south that visitors approach. At numerous small shrines and pavilions specifically set aside for the purpose visitors are required to wash their hands in a brief ritual of purification, and at the flight of steps that leads to the enclosure there is another open pavilion, sheltering a granite basin, where they again rinse their hands in clear cold water. If it is winter and they happen to be wearing western clothing they remove their overcoats. (It is rude to indicate discomfort by wearing an overcoat indoors, and in a sense the entire precinct, not the Shoden alone, is the home of Amaterasu O-mi-Kami.) The Shoden and the gates in all but the first fence lie on the same axis: to align everything perfectly would be to flaunt a perfection appropriate only to the handiwork of the spirits; so it is better, Japanese carpenters believe, to include a deliberate imperfection like an off-center gate, which also has the merit of conforming to the Japanese taste for informal, intuitively balanced composition. Between each fence is a post and lintel structure—a doorless gate—called a *torii.* The two columns of these gates are joined at the top by two horizontal members, the upper one often exceeding the actual span by several feet. The *torii* symbolizes Japanese architecture much the way a Doric capital summons up a Greek temple; but unlike a Doric capital a *torii* is an independent decorative structure whose meaning is clear and complete: it signifies a holy place. (Japan has more than 140,000 Shinto shrines, and each of them has at least one *torii.*) Strips of white silk curtain the second gate, revealing, as they flutter in the wind, another *torii* and beyond that another fence. Approaching this gate worshippers bow, clap their hands to announce themselves and attract the attention of the spirit, and then, after a few moments of silent prayer, withdraw to one side where they may admire the surrounding forest and what little may be seen, above the fence, of the sacred inner precincts. The atmosphere is calm, purposeful, but not exalted; it is rather a purification and heightening of an experience of nature accessible in Japan wherever the landscape has not been touched by industrialization. At Ise, perhaps, the landscape has an extra beauty because of the huge ancient cryptomeria. There is also a disturbing silence, broken sometimes by the abrupt sound of clapping hands and the distant thin music of temple dancing.

ISE SHRINE

The Shoden. Raised approximately 7 feet above the ground, the building stands in an enclosure entirely surfaced with white gravel. Columns and plank walls are of pale yellow *hinoki* (cypress) ; the roof is of thatch. Flame-shaped ornaments on the balustrade are red, yellow, black, and green lacquer on bronze; all other ornaments are gilt bronze. The decorative cross-piece called *chigi* and the cylindrical weights on the roof, called *katsuogi,* may once have been tie members for the ridge pole.

ISE SHRINE

The Shoden. Beams are at first supported only by the plank walls. After a year the planks will shrink and allow the beams to settle in place. Therefore a small space, visible in the photograph, is left between all columns and the beams they will eventually support. Decorative strips projecting above the ridge pole, which is carried by independent columns, are believed originally to have been hung with a number of whips signifying family rank. Bronze covers protecting the ends of the beams are of the Tokugawa age and reflect the influence of Buddhist ornamentation. The slender rafters which appear to support this roof are actually hung from beams inside the roof itself. Two thin layers of reed protect the exposed underside of the thatch, which is first dried and colored dark brown by smoking, then sewn into bundles, fastened to the structure, and trimmed to a curve prepared on wood templates. The curve, which occurs in cross-section only and not in elevation, is itself believed to be an example of Buddhist influence.

Only the Emperor and the High Priest of Ise ever enter the Shoden. For most Japanese it is not necessary to see what is hidden behind the fences. "I know not what lies within," the Priest Saigyo declared in a famous poem, "but I am in tears with gratitude." Certainly the fundamental effect of Ise's plan is its air of mystery, and the four fences which consecutively enclose the buildings are a solemn architectural version of the magic circle. Ise's buildings are a relatively late type in the evolution of Shinto architecture. *Shimmei,* its style designation, refers to modifications of earlier roof designs, the most important change being the placement of the entrance not at one side of the gable end, as it is at Izumo, but in the exact center of the long side of the building. Although they vary in size and placement each structure is almost identical in detail and spatial conception. All the buildings are essentially variations on a single architectural theme, and the effect they produce is that of a series of photographic enlargements and reductions, juxtaposed in such a way that the landscape itself seems to have been alternately stretched and condensed to accommodate a sudden shift in scale. Raised above the ground, the building type represented by the Shoden has an independent column at each of the gable ends to support the ridge pole, like the earlier *Takayuka* structures. Straight rafters carry a weight of thatch which may be considered the building's chief ornament, surpassing in the boldness of its effect even the decorative wood cylinders like logs, called *katsuogi,* placed along the ridge. (The function of these heavy cylinders may originally have been to prevent the roof from lifting in a strong wind; at Ise their shape and size have been carried beyond any purely practical purpose.) The thatch roof is sewn together in bundles, tied to the rafters, and then, with the aid of wood templates like those used in the construction of a boat, cut and trimmed to produce a gentle convex surface. The roof is, as it were, given a haircut, patted, combed, and brushed into shape.

The buildings at Ise illustrate perfectly that preference for the articulation of structural elements which has suffered only a very occasional lapse during the twenty-odd centuries of its history in Japan. But Shinto architecture's transformation of structural necessities into sculptural forms of abstract beauty is a process better described as amplification rather than articulation. For the Japanese architect merely to reveal a fact is of no great significance; to transcend the fact is to approach truth, in architecture as in religion. The truth that transcends the facts has surprising manifestations at Ise. Because Amaterasu O-mi-Kami represents the purity of nature, a building designed to shelter the sacred

ISE SHRINE
The Shoden, north elevation.

ISE SHRINE
Prayer gate in the second fence.

symbol in which the deity resides must itself embody that purity, and not in appearance only. Thus the round columns of *hinoki* (Japanese cypress) ranging in diameter from 2 feet to 4 feet, are planted directly in the ground, as they once grew, even though they immediately begin to deteriorate from dampness. Like the columns themselves, the beams, ridge pole, and rafters are often far larger than they need to be, but it is the details of joinery which suggest even more the response of the sculptor as much as of the carpenter-architect. Bold shapes whose surfaces are their sole adornment, smoothed and polished to warm the golden-yellow grain of *hinoki,* finally come to suggest, like many of the wood carvings of Constantin Brancusi, that they would look as they do if nature were suddenly to produce them.

But the effort to sustain, or rather renew, this architecture is necessarily as formidable as that which created it. Once every twenty years, since the reign of Emperor Temmu (673-686) every fence and building is completely rebuilt on an identical adjoining site. The present buildings are the fifty-ninth reconstruction. This process has by now almost depleted the Imperial forests of their reserve of suitably large *hinoki* trees, and future restorations, like the one completed in 1953, may have to draw heavily on Korean and Formosan timber supplies. Since the seventh century there have been minor modifications of the design due to the influence of Buddhism. Brass ornaments on the balustrade, the *katsuogi,* the gable ends of the Shoden, and on the fence posts, while often having a practical purpose are nevertheless of debatable authenticity. More important, perhaps, is the veranda surrounding the Shoden: probably incorporated into the design in ancient times, it makes more elegant but much less powerful the awesome forms seen in the east and west treasure houses, where the original design is maintained with greater accuracy.

Nevertheless for over twelve hundred years the symbolic youth and purity of Shinto architecture has been periodically retrieved. Each time the buildings are consecrated anew. When the work has been completed the spirit that dwells in the mirror is led from the old Shoden to a nearby shrine, where it receives offerings of food. Then the Sacred Mirror is carried back—but this time to the new Shoden—and the spirit, following, is thought not to be seriously disturbed; the new home is identical in every respect to the old one, except for its polished, golden freshness.

ISE SHRINE

West treasure house. The solid walls are planks set on edge and fitted into grooves in the columns. Similar treasure houses at Ise Geku, first built in 478 three miles distant from Ise Naiku, are fitted with steps made of massive squared logs. Both treasure houses at Ise Naiku preserve the ancient structural forms with greater vitality than does the Shoden.

East treasure house.

ISE SHRINE

Every twenty years the buildings and their enclosures are rebuilt on an adjoining site. When the new buildings (at the right) have been consecrated and the symbols in which the deity resides have been installed, the old buildings and fences will be dismantled. The latest reconstruction is the fifty-ninth over a period of twelve hundred years; the ritual will be repeated once again in 1974.

Chairs are not used in Japanese houses. Silk cushions called *zabuton* are placed directly on the mat floors. At the right is a wood armrest, called *kyosoku*. The portable charcoal brazier at the left is not used to heat a room but to warm the hands of those who sit near it. Called a *hibachi*, the brazier consists of a copper bucket set in a lacquer container.

2

Basic assumptions the Japanese make about the world they live in—both visible and invisible—are far more important to their art of architecture than are the specific qualities of materials, whether a building be made of steel and glass, wood, stone, or the earth itself. Until the intrusion of Western values the natural way to build was simply to meet the requirements of warm weather—an assumption of such seeming reasonableness to the Japanese that to debate it would have been idle. Thus for centuries the people of Japan have lived on the floors of papery pavilions not as warm as the crude earth huts of the Koreans, who long ago devised a form of central heating. Winter in Japan is less bitter than it is in Korea, but it is not so much milder that the variety of charcoal braziers used by the Japanese to warm their houses, or at least their hands, could be considered an adequate solution to the problem of heating. Winter was held to offer an experience of difficult but rewarding beauty. The wise man would not struggle to avoid it but would deliberately submit himself to it. Indeed, by the seventeenth century those adepts of Zen Buddhism who had mastered "the art of being in the world" knew how to relish the falling snow, while sitting calmly in a room thrown open to its frozen garden. Nevertheless, from September to April less philosophical Japanese are cold—not because they do not know how to make themselves warm but because they have preferred to build for summer. The demands of climate, and the availability of materials and technical skills combine to influence architectural form, but they are themselves interpreted according to those patterns of response by which a society develops all of its concepts. Religious aspirations, philosophy, and fortitude were evidently far stronger factors in shaping Japanese architecture than was, for example, the climate, and yet no architecture in the world can be described as more closely related to its environment than the architecture of Japan.

There is one other aspect of Japanese life, apart from those private and social gestures motivated by religion and philosophy, that has profoundly influenced the country's architecture. Japan is the only major civilization in the world never to have developed furniture; the Japanese prefer to sit on the floor. There are, of course, items of furniture like portable screens, boxes, chests of drawers and low tables; all of them are stored in closets when not in use. That this preference for sitting on the floor in an empty room has its origin in some deep racial tie with the hot countries, where houses as well as furniture are very nearly superfluous, is a speculation neither more nor less rewarding than that which attributes a distaste for furniture to a truly acute

The *kotatsu* provides more warmth than does the *hibachi*. It consists of a charcoal brazier with a removable wood grille set over it like a table. To store heat a heavy quilt is spread over the *kotatsu* and the legs of the people sitting around it. Another version of the *kotatsu* is entirely built into the floor; a mattress placed near it, with a quilt long enough to cover both the *kotatsu* and the mattress, makes a comfortable sleeping arrangement.

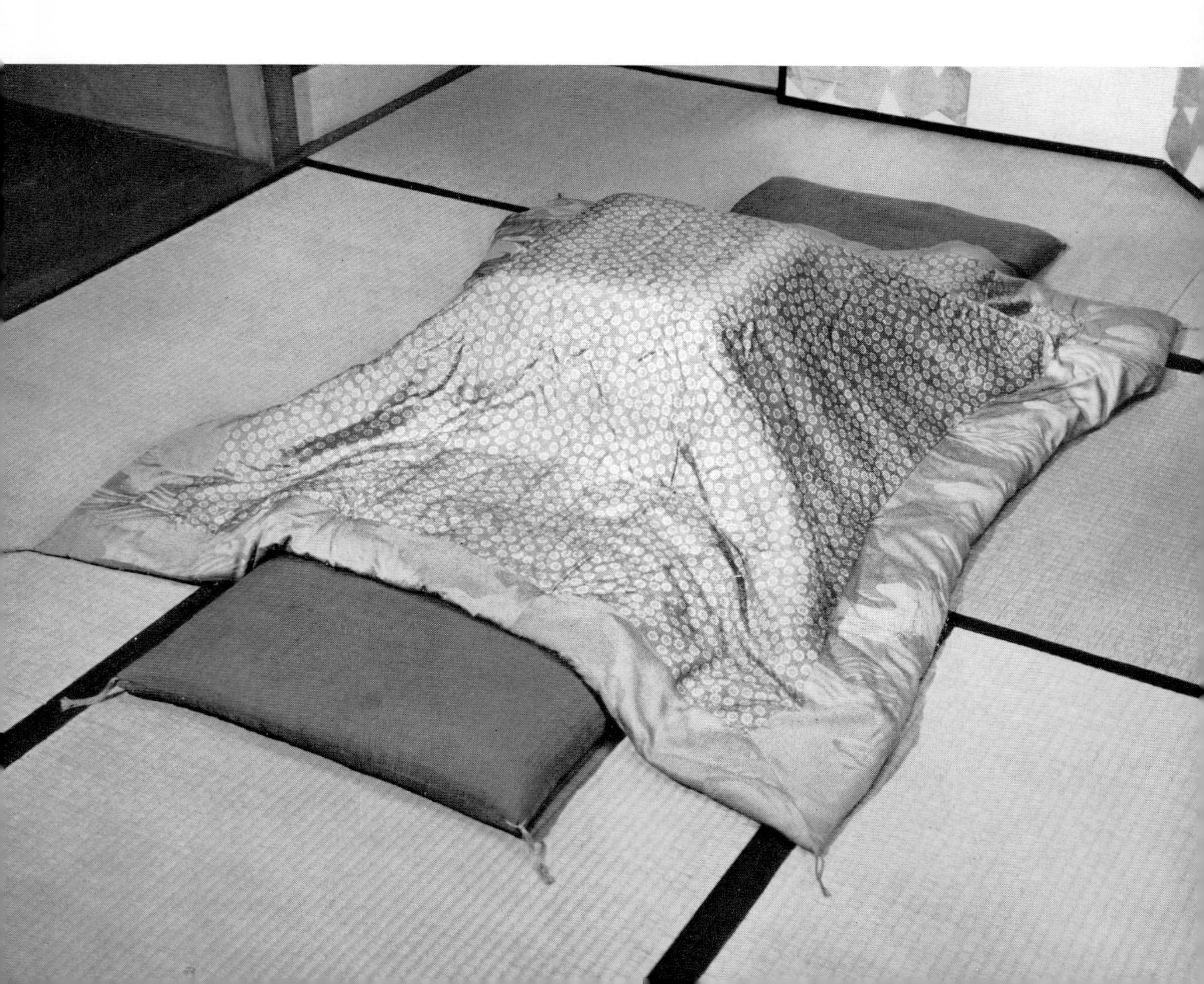

fastidiousness. But the practical results of sitting on the floor can be strictly measured. It has influenced the choice of materials and textures, besides making it desirable to build the floor off the ground; it has influenced the design of clothing and made absolutely necessary the removal of shoes before entering a building, since the floor itself is a kind of fragile furniture; it has influenced the size of rooms, which may conveniently be small if they are to accommodate people only; it has encouraged the use of moveable partitions, often decorated with large paintings since there is nothing to obstruct either the view of such partitions or access to them; and it has influenced the design of gardens, which are seen most often by eyes approximately 2 feet 6 inches above the floor. In China one rises from the comfort of a chair to greet one's guests; in Japan one kneels on the floor. Servants in many restaurants and homes still enter a room on their knees, as does the mistress of the house when meeting her conservative husband's friends, although the change in daily living habits due to the introduction of Western ways, particularly in business life, has brought about the collapse through sheer unwieldiness of many such customs.

Between the primitive impulse to architectural form manifested by the Yayoi pit dwellings, and the highly developed abstractions of structure at Izumo and Ise, two themes are established: the characteristic Japanese sense of construction emerges in the process of fitting together many separate pieces of wood to outline space with a structural cage; and the Japanese sense of shelter is expressed by amplifying the roof into a faceted sculpture. The skeleton frame and the dense roof which tops it are, to the Japanese form sense, decisive architectural elements, and such separate disciplines as orientation, plan, structure, and decoration, achieve their happiest effects when they facilitate this form sense. It is convenient first to consider these elements apart from the social influences which produced specific building types and their local variations. Separated, for the moment, from such details, the form itself may be examined with an eye to discovering by what inner laws it evolves.

A significant problem of design for the carpenter-architects of Ise would have been an irrelevant detail for the men who built, say, the Parthenon—although the Greeks preserved in stone many of the forms they originally developed in wood construction. The Greeks found meaningful architecture in a just equilibrium of parts, ordering podium, columns, and roof in a composition made incoherent if any one of those elements unjustly dominated the others. The builders of medieval cathedrals elevated the dynamics of thrust and counter-thrust to a pre-eminence which ultimately destroyed the sense of supporting and supported members. In Europe's renaissance a reappraisal of the Mediterranean tradition established the wall as an architectural factor of decisive significance; the roof, except as a dome, frequently disappeared altogether, leaving only a cornice to show where it had been. Even in the twentieth century, when skeleton-frame construction in steel or concrete has brought about a reappraisal of all the elements of architectural composition, the Western architect habitually composes a building with walls—facades. But for the Japanese the most expressive architectural element has always been the roof. A Japanese building *is* a roof, and when the Japanese speak of the beauty of a building they think at once of the proportions, the curvature, the sculptural modeling, and the texture of its roof because here the architect reveals his particular sensitivity, especially in buildings of monumental size, through adjustments of extraordinary delicacy.

Four types of roof have been developed and refined by the Japanese over the centuries. They are the single gable, called *Kirizuma;* the square pyramidal, called *Hogyo;* the hipped roof, called *Yosemune* or *Shichu;* and the *Irimoya,* a Japanese combination of the hipped and gabled roofs. Variations of this last type are found also in the southern Pacific islands, and the prototypes for all of them may be found in China.

Although skilled carpenters may dispense with full-scale dress rehearsals, quite often wood members for each of these roof types are first assembled on the ground, with wedges and tenons. After important corrections have been made the structure is dismantled and set aside, each piece having been numbered. Respectable craftsmanship requires that all parts which remain visible when the roof is completed be pasted over with thin paper to protect the surface from fingermarks; the wood is not painted but is rubbed with a vegetable oil which, in time, darkens its golden tone to a rich deep brown. Immediately following completion of the column structure, and before the walls have been filled in, the roof is constructed in place. The framework for a roof 60 feet by 40 feet can be assembled by ten men in about two days. Some of the beams may consist of entire tree trunks, rough-hewn, but assembly begins with the finished pieces, often of a purely decorative nature, which appear to support the overhanging eaves. When the ridge pole is in place a religious ceremony called *Mune-age* is held to insure by divine protection the safety and durability of the whole building, and to give thanks for the safe completion of the difficult part of the work.

Considering the weight of tile or thatch loaded onto the

ROOF TYPES

Top row, left: *Kirizuma*. Right: *Hogyo*. Bottom row, left: *Shichu*. Right: *Irimoya*.

In temple compounds or groups of palace buildings roof types were arranged hierarchically, *Shichu* and *Irimoya* roofs being generally reserved for larger and more important buildings.

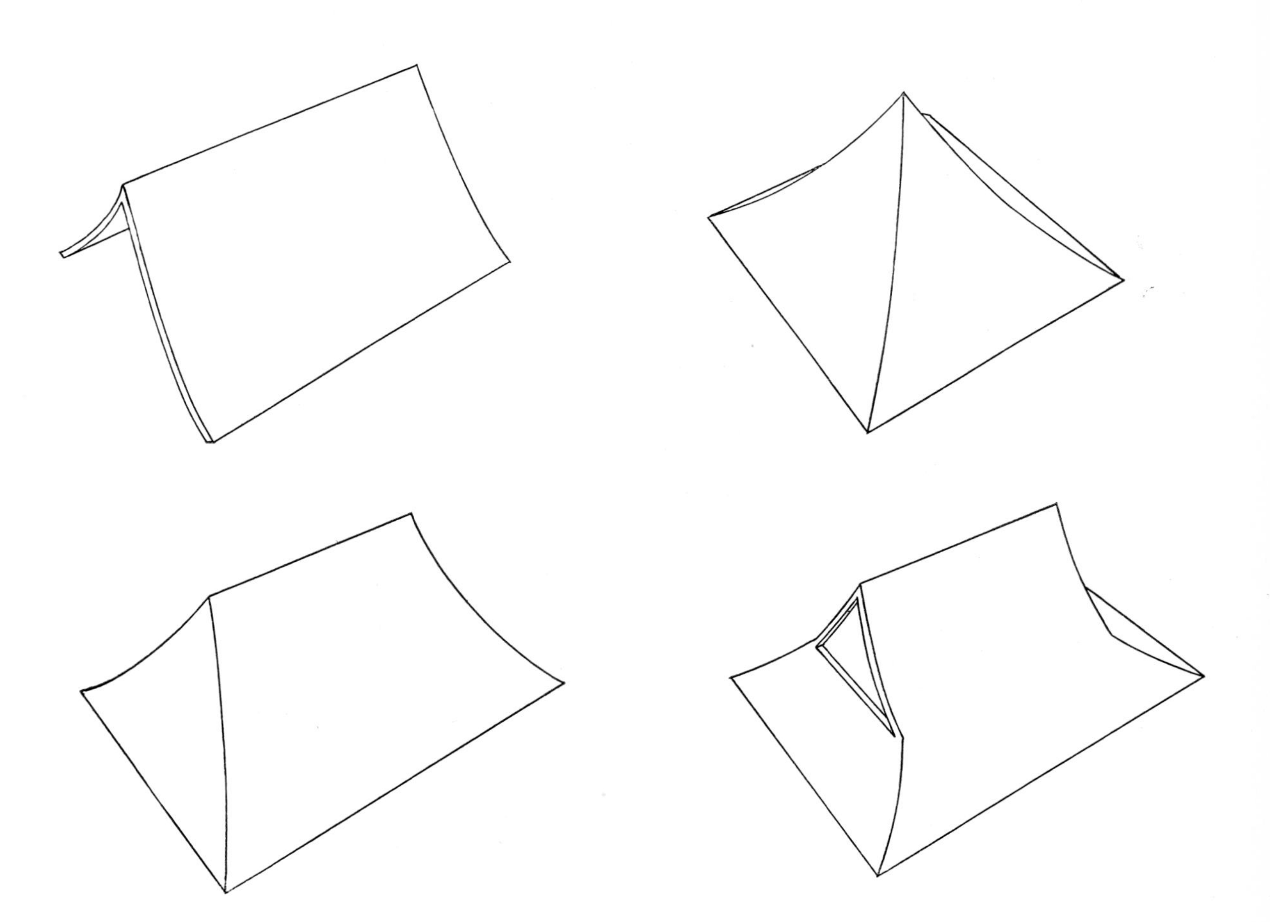

roofs of Japanese houses the Western achitect would expect to discover that a considerable ingenuity had been expended in the development of strong and economical framing techniques. But such an expectation would be gratified instead by the discovery that Japanese carpenters succeed in balancing massive superstructures by techniques unconcerned with those elementary principles of the truss that have effectively operated in all the techniques of timber construction known to Western practice. The adequacy of the Japanese methods is proved by Todaiji temple's Kondo, the largest wood building in the world. What keeps the roof of a Japanese building in place, first of all, is its enormous weight. It rests on the columns like a granite table top; the more heavily the table is loaded, Japanese carpenters assert, the more secure it is. Earthquakes succeed only in making the whole building bounce and sway, because the columns perch on stones at ground level, rather than on deep sunken foundations. But nevertheless a sudden severe shock brings tile tumbling into the street, and sometimes the rest of the roof follows. The principle of the truss is not unknown to the Japanese, and is indeed widely used in today's Westernized practice. But until now it has been distasteful to the Japanese sense of form. In the same way the Greeks, knowing the principle of the arch, reserved its use mainly for sewers. While such discriminations are not necessarily rational they are motivated nevertheless by a consistent logic of values. Thus the Japanese, seeking to preserve the cage-like purity of horizontal and vertical members, construct the roof with heavy horizontal beams carrying many vertical posts. Sometimes, if the beams are to be hidden by a flat suspended ceiling, a few of them will be made from naturally curved tree trunks, taking advantage of the extra strength provided by the slight arch. The lowest beams are supported by columns at both ends, and the vertical posts they carry are placed close to the columns to reduce the bending moment of the beams as much as possible. There may be as many tiers of beams and vertical posts as are considered necessary to ensure adequate strength; occasionally these beautiful constructions reach a startling complexity, requiring such quantities of timber as to dissuade engineers whose technology is less lavish from attempting to design them.

Any of the four roof types, individually or in combination, may be found suitable for a particular building, but certain of them are more obviously suited to simple problems. For example, the square pyramidal roof lends itself very well to smaller buildings, and is often used for temples and houses of limited size and extreme simplicity of plan. A gable roof, less intricate than those found in Shinto

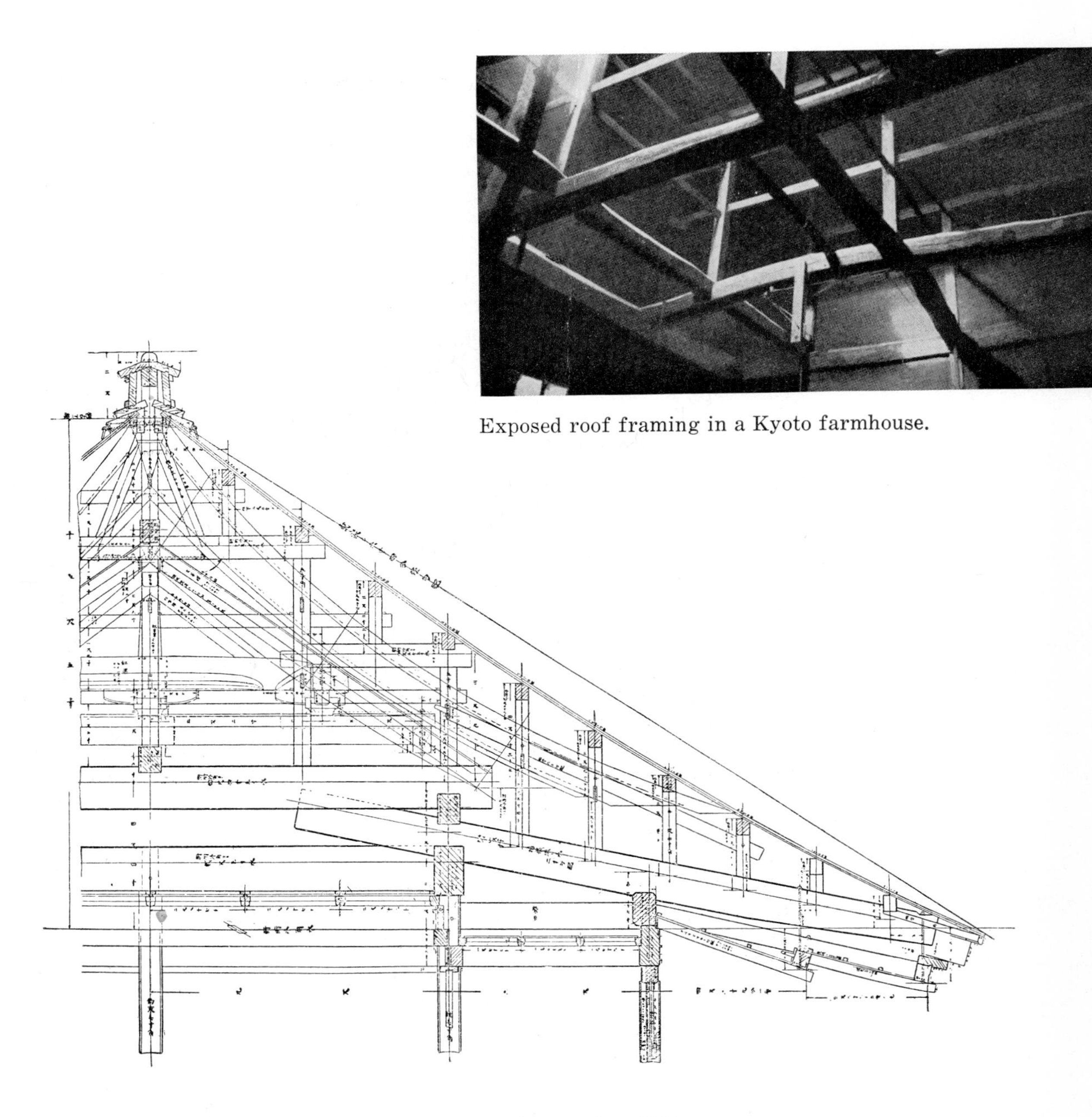

Exposed roof framing in a Kyoto farmhouse.

Cross-section of roof framing. From a carpenter's manual c. 1860.

Posts of varying height are supported by heavy beams. (Those shown in the photograph take advantage of the natural curve of the tree.) Cantilevered roof members are fastened between two beams well toward the center of the building. These members also support a series of posts and beams which carry a thin board sheathing and tiles or shingles. (The straight line in the drawing indicates the degree of pitch and also reveals the amount of curvature.) Projecting approximately 8 feet beyond the exterior wall, the rough beams are covered with false rafters both to provide a finished surface and to make the roof appear still thicker.

shrines, is by virtue of its relative structural simplicity used most often for farmhouses, barns, or other buildings where, regardless of their place in the hierarchy of social preference, an air of unassuming modesty seems appropriate. But more complicated forms also lend themselves to small buildings. The main building of Murōji Temple, near Nara, is in all respects a modest structure except for the extravagant grace of its *Irimoya* roof. The curved eaves line, called *sori,* is here the Japanese modification of the more emphatically curved roofs introduced into Japan from China, during the seventh century, as a detail necessary to temple architecture. Like the gable roof, the hipped roof is proper to a rectangular plan, and the two forms are often combined in private houses ranging from the very modest to the elaborate mansions of feudal dignitaries. In its purest form, that is to say when it covers a single rectangular unit, the *Irimoya* roof mitigates a too sharp distinction between front and sides of a building, and the problem of carrying off a heavy rainfall often suggests to the designer solutions of great plastic and pictorial interest. When a large building, with several wings arrayed in echelon, asymmetrically, is tied together by a series of *Irimoya* roofs, their intersections become most complicated and are a chief source of invention for those pictorial effects—best seen from one preferred angle—that so much delight the Japanese connoisseur.

Roof coverings of tile or thatch, singly or in combination, are generally used for farmhouses. Tile is appropriate for more elaborate Buddhist temples and for private houses, both in the country and in town. Of the various kinds of tile used two are seen most often. Imported from China, the oldest of these designs is called *hongawara.* It consists of concave tiles overlapped by convex pieces which provide a watertight cover. The design produces an emphatically striped texture, as if the roof were made of widely spaced bamboo poles. The less expensive of the traditional tile designs consists of single pieces convex at one end and concave at the other; no intermediate pieces are required. A tile roof is built up on thin boards applied to the rafters. The boards are covered with a layer of shingles and then with a thick layer of mud or clay. Tiles are often embedded in this mud without any other bonding agent, so that in time their hold on the roof is precarious. But on more elaborately executed roofs the tiles are wired to each other and to the boarding.

For temples and private houses, as well as for tea ceremony houses, shingles made from the bark of *hinoki* or *sawara* trees produce a roof the chief esthetic merit of which is its *teri,* or sheen. These shingle roofs are designed

MURŌJI TEMPLE

Shingled with *hinoki* bark, the *Irimoya* roof of Murōji Temple, near Nara, is distinguished for its unusually subtle curvature. Chains attached to the ridge provide a means of access. The ridge is covered with copper sheets.

The thatched *Irimoya* roof of this farmhouse near Kyoto is combined with a tile roof to protect the veranda. The ridge is decorated with bamboo poles; such decorations vary in each province. According to sound practice a thatch roof must have at least a 45° slope, with considerably more preferred in the northern provinces.

Thatch and two traditional tile designs are combined in the gable roof of this farmhouse at Nara. The small tile roof at the right covers a chimney.

MYOSHINJI TEMPLE

The elaborate tile ornaments, reflecting Chinese influence, are designed to emphasize the roof's flamboyant, ascending curves. Dolphins, symbolizing water, are placed at both ends of the ridge to protect the building from fire. The intersections of the eaves are equipped with grimacing horned heads to ward off evil spirits.

KITANO TENJIN SHRINE

Hinoki bark shingles are used for the main roof and the seven modified *Irimoya* roofs clustered around it. Although the shingles average 8 inches at the eaves, the actual thickness over most of the roof surface is 1 inch. Ridges are sheathed in copper; the wave-pattern end pieces are of tile.

Two hipped roofs are superimposed in this Kyoto house. The lower roof, called *engawa,* covers the veranda. Both roofs employ slight convex curves in a Japanese departure from the concave surfaces and more pronounced curves characteristic of Chinese roof designs. The thickness of the shingles at the eaves only is 2 inches; the actual thickness is less than 1 inch.

with great subtlety. For example, because a good part of its beauty consists of a simple quantitative display of thousands of bark shingles along the eaves, this section is sometimes made three or four times as thick as the actual weatherproof covering on the rest of the roof. In reality it is an artificial rim designed to suggest that the entire roof is quite thick and heavy: but only that part which overhangs the rafters at the eaves line actually has such thickness, and to sustain the illusion it often becomes necessary to suspend false rafters below the real ones. On the other hand, an entirely different effect is obtained by revealing, or even reducing, the actual thickness of the shingles at the eaves line, so that by their very thinness the eaves belie the real weight of the superstructure. Both treatments can be modified for different effects by rounding the edges of the eaves, especially where its line is long and gently curved, or by cutting the edges as sharply as possible, with the fascia sloping abruptly inward toward the walls.

Those vast, hat-like roofs are made to hover above the fields by constructions that seem only indifferently concerned with what they support. But the skeleton frame of wood is the inner discipline of Japanese architecture, and it is the physical outline of a conception of space. The placement of isolated column supports is determined by two considerations: the practical limits imposed by the scale of a particular building and by the available sizes of timber; and by the desire to make of the space contained in a building a series of finite units, in theory if not in practice capable of unlimited extension. Space in Japanese architecture is additive. A room is a closed volume adjoined by other closed volumes. Though they may vary in scale, they are seldom intended to express those over-riding preoccupations of the Western architect with spatial sequences progressing from minor to major. Japanese architectural space characteristically knows no beginning, middle, and end.

The preference for additive space is revealed not only in Japanese architecture itself but in the way buildings are represented in Japanese painting. A view into the many rooms of a house is often taken above normal eye level, so that the observer seems to be peering down on the scene while sitting in a tree. From such a vantage point one would expect only an excellent view of the roof. But the conventions of Japanese pictorial representation permit the roof to be omitted entirely, so that instead one looks down on a cluster of cells partitioned like a tray of ice cubes. The nearest facade is sometimes drawn parallel to the picture plane, and the lines indicating the sides of the building and its interior partitions are drawn in isometric perspective. This method requires that all lines which in reality are parallel to each other be drawn just that way. As a consequence Japanese perspective, like that of other Eastern cultures, does not depend on a vanishing point toward which all lines converge to create the illusion of depth. Without a vanishing point the representation of a building and its various rooms may be extended indefinitely, and in the scroll paintings called *e-makimono* buildings are often extended for several feet without the drawing being organized, as a composition, around any single dominating element. Thus the conventions of painting and perspective present a house as an aggregate of rectangular spaces, strictly delimited and often so alike as to be interchangeable.

In architecture itself no less than in pictures of architecture, differences in quality or mood, or purpose, are expressed through the size of a particular room and through the richness of its appointments. But there is nothing in the disposition of the rooms or in the treatment of space itself to suggest that a building has been imagined in its entirety according to some preconceived abstract hierarchy of spatial experiences. In the view which regards architecture as a kind of music, Japanese architecture is a thoughtful meandering along a keyboard. Each note struck is another column; the intervals of silence are the spaces they delimit. Crescendos are rare, the art of the fugue is unknown, and to the Western observer there seems to be no reason why this architectural "music" can not continue forever across the landscape.

Each of the volumes which together comprise a house reveal the identical discipline of design. In order to trace this discipline in its various manifestations, from foundation stones to mural decorations, it is preferable to consider first the simple units of measurement by which the discipline is imposed.

The Japanese unit of measurement is the *shaku.* One *shaku* corresponds to 11.93 inches, and is itself divided into 10 *sun.* Six *shaku* constitute 1 *ken,* which is the basic linear unit of measurement in architectural planning. Lumber is prepared in standard lengths of 1, 1½, 2, and 2½ *ken.* A square the sides of which measure one *ken* constitutes an area of one *tsubo;* this area is the basic unit of measurement for surfaces. Buildings are considered to cover so many *tsubo,* rather than square *shaku* or *ken* of floor space. But a basic unit of measurement in the east of Japan is not the same thing in the west of Japan. When the capital was established at Nara in the eighth century, with its streets organized in a right-angled grid, the *ken* was a 6 foot unit designating the distance between columns. In eastern Japan,

KASUGA GONGEN SCROLL

Kamakura, c. 1300. (detail) Collection Imperial Household Museum, Tokyo.

The rooms of a palace are shown with the roof and the upper part of the walls removed. Partitions at floor level are sliding paper screens decorated with landscape paintings (right). Fine bamboo curtains, called *sudari,* are shown rolled up at the top of the columns (left, center) and unrolled along the exterior walls (foreground). Above the *sudari* are wood weather doors hinged at the top and suspended from the eaves.

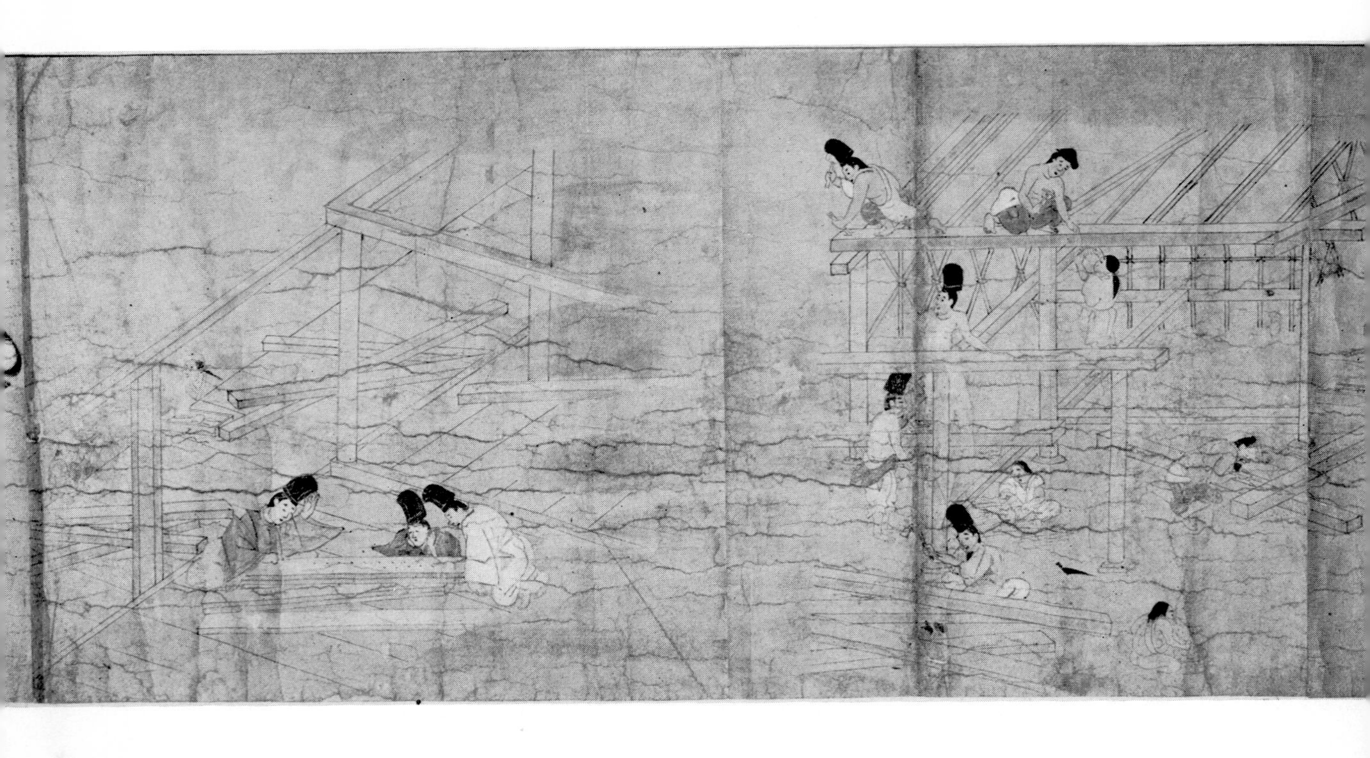

TENJIN ENGI SCROLL

Kamakura, thirteenth century. (detail) Collection Metropolitan Museum of Art, New York.

Carpenters, wearing hats of lacquered cloth, are shown constructing a temple. A light bamboo scaffold can be seen in the background at the right.

and particularly in Edo, the seventeenth century capital of the Tokugawa Shoguns, the *ken* designated a space from the center of one column to the center of the next. In addition to these local divergences in method, there are other differences due to fine distinctions between the relative importance of buildings. Thus in Kyoto a *ken* when applied to a mansion meant 7 feet, or 6 feet 6 inches for a temple, or 6 feet 3 inches for a house—and there were many other variations not traceable to any single cause. By the end of the fifteenth century the *ken* was considered a fixed unit of measure, although Kyoto and Edo (Tokyo) distinctions persist to this day.

Ordinarily columns along the exterior walls of a building are not placed closer together than one *ken*. A wall 3 *ken* long—approximately 18 feet—may have four columns (one at each end and two in between) but the wall opposite, which may be in the interior of the building, need not have columns that correspond in number or placement. This seemingly paradoxical freedom in the disposition of columns is an important aspect of Japanese planning. Differences in column spacing on the various walls of a room are usually produced by the juxtaposition of two or more rooms of different sizes. Two small rooms backed up on one larger room necessarily reveal an intermediate column on one wall of the larger room, since columns are ordinarily exposed on both sides of a wall. Another, and perhaps the most obvious, effect of spacing columns irregularly is to stress one particular opening in a wall; by omitting one of the four columns on a hypothetical 3 *ken* wall, the resulting larger interval focuses attention on the view outside, even if the view through the narrower adjoining bay is left unobstructed.

Foundations for the columns are provided by small stones. A cylindrical recess in the top of each stone receives a peg cut out of the bottom of each column; no connection less tenuous than this keeps a Japanese building in place, and the foundation stones, carefully set in a bed of rock and gravel, perhaps 2 feet deep, seem never to shift and settle. About 2 feet above the ground each column is joined to a floor beam. There are no basements, but sometimes the space between the ground and the floor is enclosed by a plaster wall to keep stray animals from establishing themselves underneath the house. Numerous columns underneath the floor beams provide additional support and make the floors of Japanese houses unusually sturdy. There are, in fact, really two sets of columns: those which support both floor and roof beams, and those which support the floor beams alone. Verandas and overhanging roofs receive their own complement of columns. Like other exposed wood members, all of these columns are usually left in their natural state:

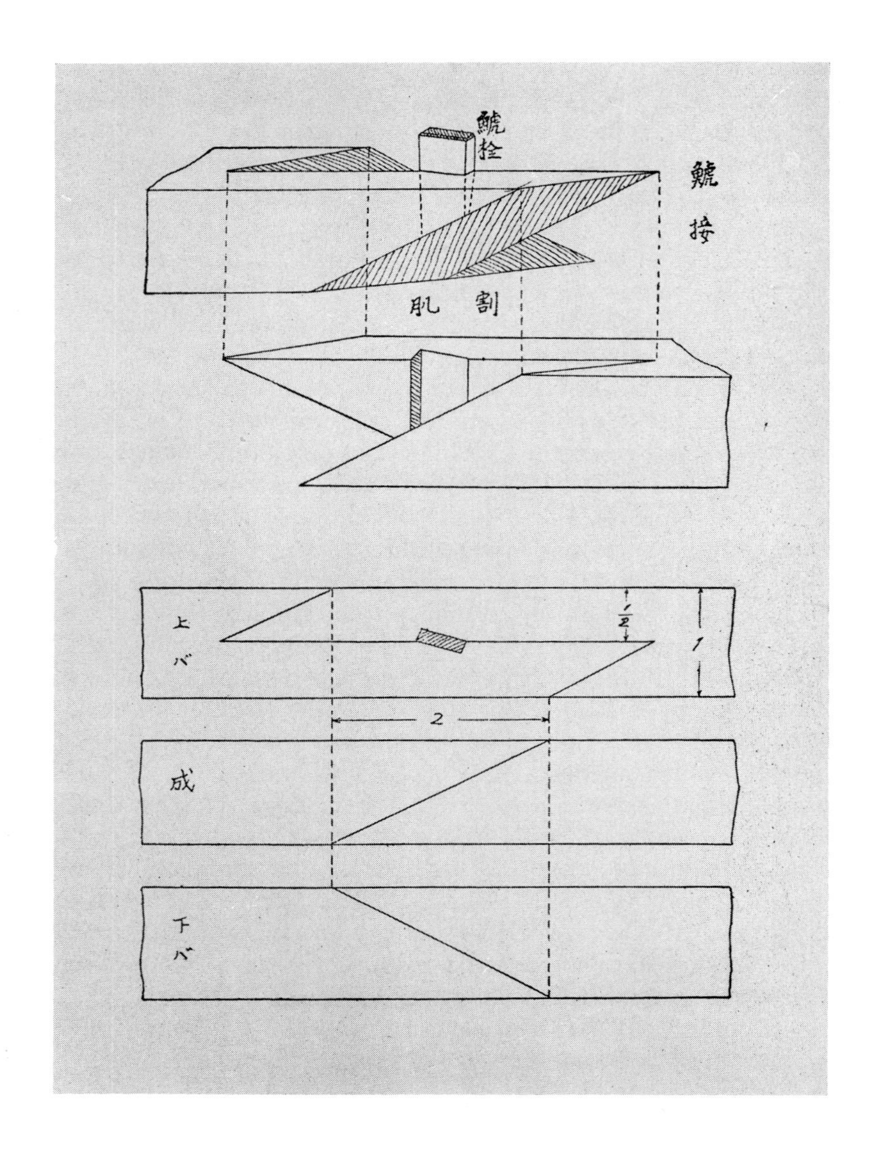

Detail from a contemporary carpenter's manual

Connection of two exposed horizontal members. The diagonal joint is preferred because it minimizes interruption of the pattern of wood graining.

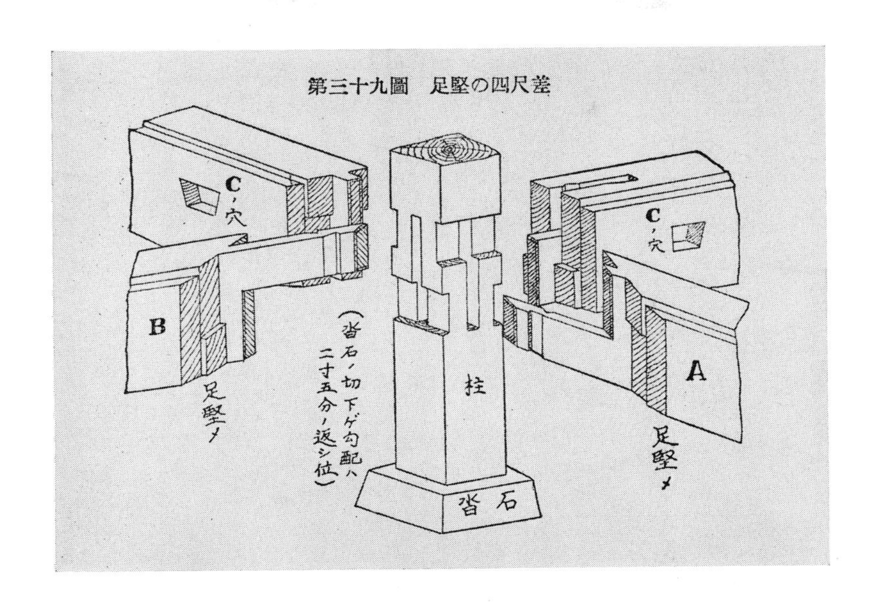

Detail from a contemporary carpenter's manual
A column cut to receive four interlocking floor beams.

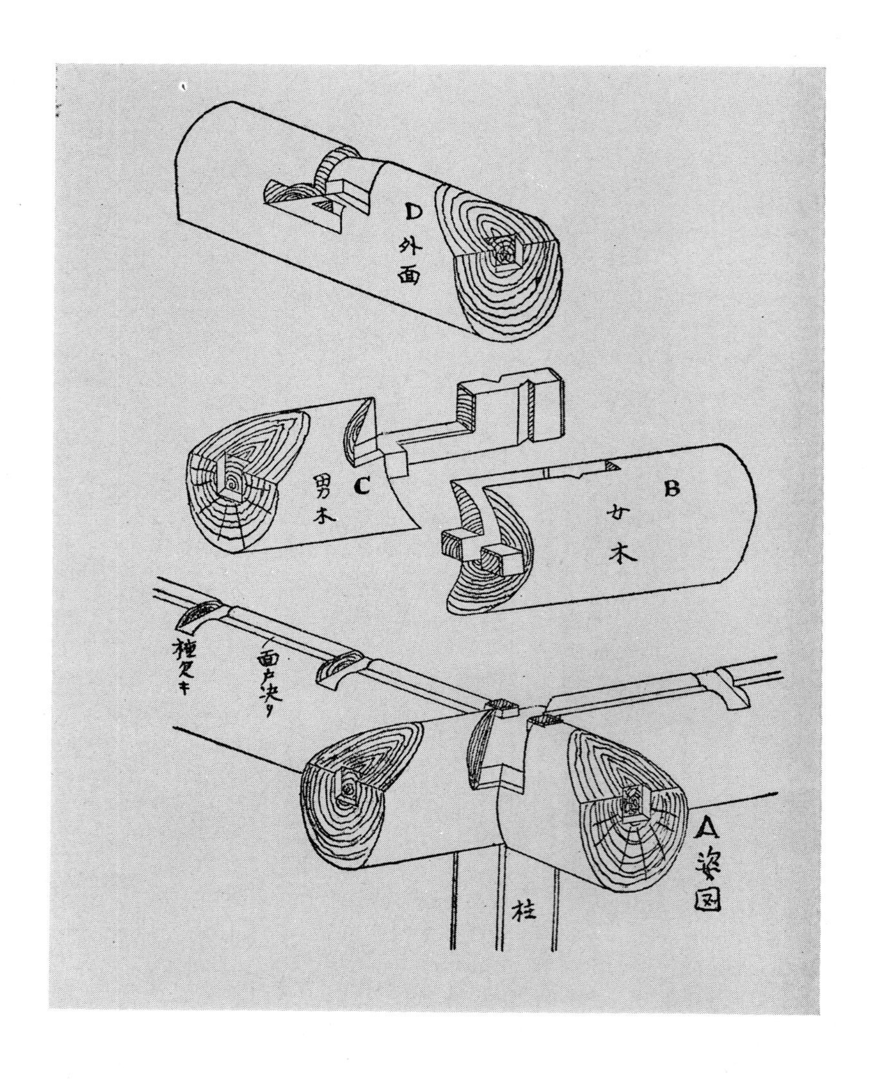

Detail from a contemporary carpenter's manual

Two round beams intersecting at a corner column. A third piece is added to make the beams appear to pass through each other. Ends of both projecting pieces are notched to receive rafters.

no paint is used, but applications of vegetable oil afford some protection against the effects of weather.

Columns are only one element in the linear description of space with which Japanese architecture is concerned. But the related structural and non-structural elements that fall within this linear discipline must be viewed in conjunction with the wall surfaces spread between them. Walls in Japanese architecture are screens against the weather, and have no structural function other than to support themselves. Since the eaves may project beyond the walls as much as 8 feet, the walls are usually well protected from rain. A solid wall is most often built up on a lath of bamboo strips tied together with rice straw fibres. Over this are applied, in two layers of slightly different consistency, a coating of mud always one half the thickness of the column (which may be from 4 to 5½ inches square), and to this is applied one finishing coat of plaster about 1/16 inch thick. This top coat of plaster is often of a paper-smooth texture comparable to that of the plaster walls used inside Western houses; in Japan the same material and the same smooth finish is used for both interior and exterior surfaces. Both the mud base and the plaster top coat are let into grooves in the columns, allowing for shrinkage without additional trim details. Craftsmanship of the best quality calls for the insertion of straw fibres taped and nailed into the groove in the column, to provide an additional bonding agent inside the wall itself. The elimination of all visible trim details wherever wood and plaster are joined produces an elegance and precision impossible to achieve by more cumbersome, if more durable, Western techniques.

By the eleventh century moveable wall panels of wood were widely used; prior to that time solid walls were built of broad planks set on edge, horizontally, as in the buildings at Ise. The moveable panels, called *shitomido,* were hinged at the top so that they could be swung up into a room and hooked to metal rods suspended from the ceiling. Occasionally they were lifted outwards and held in place by rods suspended from the eaves. Gradually these hinged doors were replaced by an arrangement of considerably greater convenience. Sliding doors of wood, called *amado,* protected sliding panels made of light wood strips to which sheets of translucent rice paper were pasted on the side exposed to the weather. Called *shoji,* these paper walls admit an agreeably cool and diffused light. In warm weather *amado* may be stored in a kind of closet attached to each exterior wall of a building, and *shoji,* on the rare occasions when they are removed, are stacked inside the building or in a separate storehouse. The smallest length of space in which *shoji* can

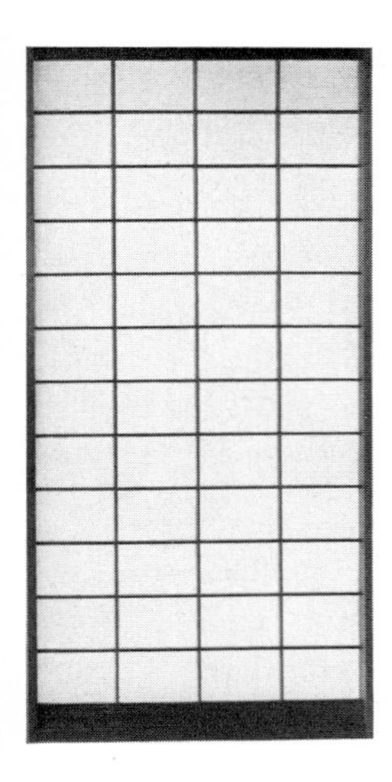

Left: a *shoji* panel with a protecting plate at the base. Translucent paper is pasted to the outer side. Proportions of the grid, made of thin wood strips, are variable. The baseplate may be omitted or, as in the earliest versions of *shoji,* only the top half of the panel may be of paper. Designed by Sutemi Horiguchi.
Right: a *fusuma* panel with black lacquer frame and inset finger-grip. Layers of opaque paper are pasted to both sides of the wood grid, which resembles that of the *shoji.* Both panels are approximately 6 feet high.

Tatami, rice straw mats covered with woven rush, average 3 feet by 6 feet and are at least 2 inches thick. The long sides are bound with black cloth tape.

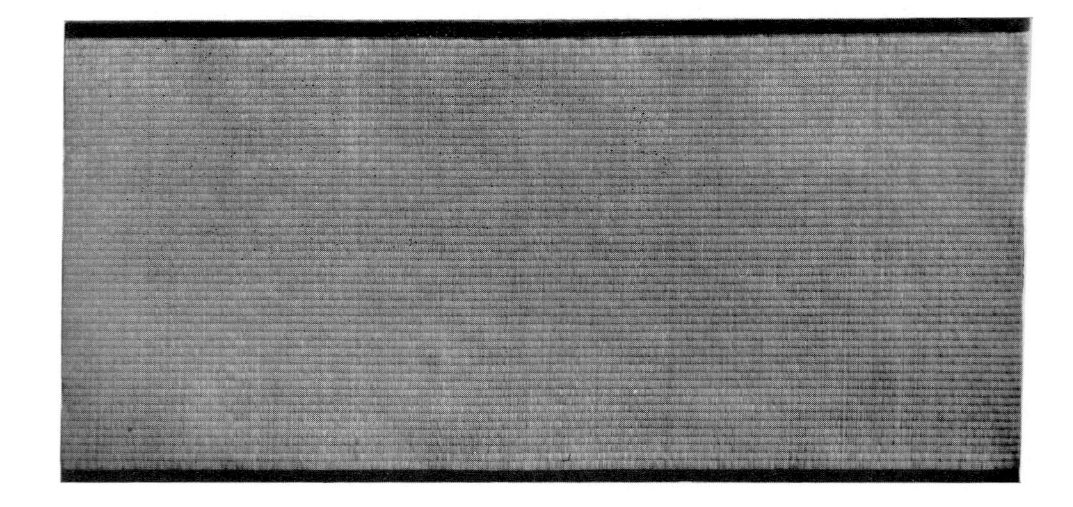

be used before their proportions become too narrow is 1 *ken,* which takes two sliding units.

Almost all partitions inside a building are made of light sliding panels similar to *shoji,* except that they are covered with heavy, opaque paper on both sides. Called *fusuma,* these interior partitions can be completely removed to convert the many rooms of a house into one open space. Often the paper used for *fusuma* is embossed with small gold or silver designs. In the great sixteenth-century efflorescence of palace and temple building *fusuma* carried a weight of mural painting in black ink, or in color on a gold or silver ground, that may be said to surpass in its subtlety and its invention the greatest achievements of architectural decoration in the Italian Renaissance. The proportions of *fusuma* are of course determined by the placement of interior columns; but quite often the process is reversed and a preference for a certain proportion will decide the placement of columns. For example, given an average height of 1 *ken,* a distance of 3 or 3½ *ken* between columns can be divided into four *fusuma* the proportions of which are generally considered to be desirable.

Even if every exterior wall of a building is composed of sliding *shoji,* unless half of them are opened the rooms will be surprisingly dark. This is due in part to the broad overhang of the eaves, but it is also, of course, an intrinsic limitation of the rice paper itself, and is further aggravated by the planning device of completely interior rooms with no source of light (or ventilation) other than that borrowed from adjoining rooms. The general gloom is compensated by the even diffusion of light, the absence of glare, and by the contrast of wood columns against white-toned walls—a contrast the pursuit of which has encouraged further clarification of interior structural detailing. Light as a controlling factor in the creation of space has played no great part in Japanese architecture, as it has, say, in the buildings of Bernini and Borromini, although a strong sense of the *quality* of light has guided much of the design and the choice of materials.

The floor also contributes to the structural organization of a building, although originally it did not have such importance. In the private rooms of Kyoto's eighth century Imperial Palace, for example, the floor was of polished *hinoki* planks with only a thick mat of rice straw bound with silk tape provided for the Emperor's particular comfort. Proportions of rooms and the placement of columns was then conditioned by elements other than an occasional floor mat. But by the middle of the fourteenth century the use of floor mats of standard sizes had spread at least to the middle and upper classes, and except in verandas, both open and closed, finished floors were now entirely of mats. Called *tatami,* these mats are made of rice straw closely packed inside a cover of woven rush. The long sides are bound with linen tape, usually black, though for special purposes a figured or printed colored silk may be used. *Tatami* average 2⅛ inches in thickness, 6 feet in length, and 3 feet in width—the latter two dimensions being conditioned by the *kyo* and *ma* systems of measuring, respectively, between columns or from center to center. Although the mat size, like every other dimension in a building, was originally determined by the standard *ken* unit of measurement, once the mat became a fixed item of the Japanese plan it acted to determine that plan more effectively than any other element. Thus the architect builds up the shape of a room by combining mats in arrangements which yield a limited number of room dimensions. In fact, rooms are described in terms of the number of mats they contain, rather than by their dimensions in *tsubo* or *ken.* Certain arrangements require half-mats, or mats of otherwise unusual size, but the standard room sizes are generally based on 4½, 6, 8, 10, 12, 15 and 18 mat combinations.

There are two great advantages to this module system. First, it guarantees an internal order and consistency to the various parts of a building. Second, because it is not based on structural elements but acts instead to organize the structure, it is a planning device of considerably greater flexibility than is at first apparent. In effect it is two modules: 1 *ken* in length and ½ *ken* in width. Simply by having one row of mats at right angles to all the others, or by arranging all the mats in a spiral pattern resembling a Greek key design, the architect avails himself of two interlocking scales. Floor patterns made by the black tape bindings are one of the most striking details of Japanese interiors. If the floor is imagined as an abstract picture composed of rectangles, it will be seen that divisions on the "frame" enclosing the picture—the walls of the room—are affected by the floor pattern itself. The black lines dividing the floor surface not only suggest to the architect the placement of columns and those intervals of *shoji* which will best relate a room to its garden, but also tie together wall and floor in a harmony as varied as it is consistent.

Besides the plan module imposed by *tatami,* two other details also contribute to the organization of wall surfaces and columns. The columns are in fact only the vertical elements of a visible structure conceived somewhat like a jungle-gym, and though it is true that they dominate the composition by their relatively unalterable performance in the linear description of space, they do not altogether escape

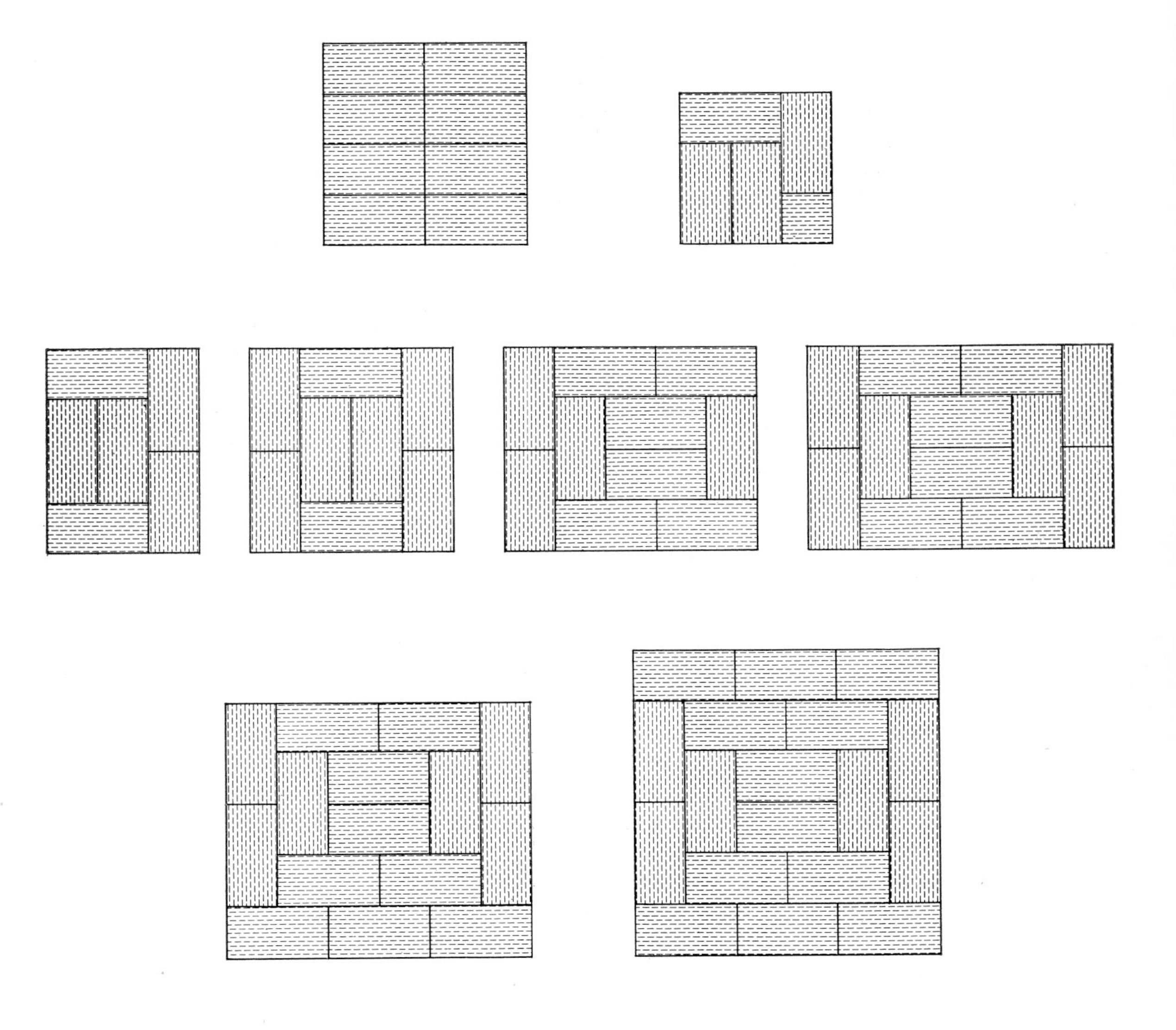

Tatami may be arranged in varying patterns to produce rooms of different sizes.

Top row: Left: eight mats arranged in the old formal style usually reserved for temples, palaces, or aristocratic mansions. Right: four and one-half mats, usually used for tea ceremony rooms. A wood panel may be substituted for the half mat.

Middle row: Six, eight, ten, and twelve mat rooms. The mats are arranged to avoid the intersection of four lines.

Bottom row: Fifteen and eighteen mat rooms. The pattern may be extended indefinitely, but the proportions of a room will be limited to those shapes produced by mat combinations which avoid four intersecting lines.

modification by the horizontal elements of the structural frame. It is just these horizontal units of structure and decoration that most subtly establish scale in Japanese interiors. Approximately 1 *ken* above the floor a beam called *nageshi,* apparently as heavy and solid as the columns it ties together, provides a continuous horizontal line around the room, like a cornice or a dado. Tracks to receive *shoji* or *fusuma* are incorporated in the *nageshi* where required. The *nageshi* is always revealed on both sides of a wall, even in fixed plaster walls where it does not function as the top framing for sliding panels. The space above the *nageshi* is usually from 18 inches to 3 feet high. It may be filled in by white plaster or *shoji,* if it is on an exterior wall, or, if it is part of an interior partition, by plaster or by a wood lattice called a *ramma.* This decorative element ranges from simple vertical grilles to the most elaborate carved filagrees of plants, animals, and birds. While the openness of the *ramma* is designed to permit circulation of air, the practical motivation for the *nageshi* itself is the provision of that lateral bracing which walls of paper or plaster do not afford. But the restriction of such bracing to horizontal elements alone is a procedure, like the characteristically devious framing of the roof, that cannot be justified on rational grounds alone. Prior to contemporary practice, in which expediency often triumphs over national taste, diagonal bracing was occasionally put to use; but it was invariably concealed within the thickness of a plaster wall. Thus the elevations of a building include horizontal bracing which forms, in conjunction with the column structure, those Mondrian-like patterns so greatly admired by contemporary Western architects. They have always been admired by the Japanese; so much so that Japanese carpenter-architects have not hesitated to introduce a superfluous "structural" element, or to conceal the presence of real ones, if by so doing they could improve the asymmetric composition of a facade.

As Japanese architecture clarified its conception of space modulated by a structural cage, the horizontal elements of the cage received still greater attention. For example, the *nageshi,* ostensibly only a practical device, is scaled far beyond its practical requirements. Made to look like a solid beam, it is in reality merely a thin grooved plank (to receive the sliding screens) flanked by two boards to strengthen it. When it spans 3 or more *ken,* the *nageshi* is often divided into two lengths. These sections are caught at the center by a post hung from the beams; the dimensions of this post are slightly smaller than those of the normal columns. Overscaling the *nageshi* guarantees that the eye will interpret it as a structural element at least as significant as the col-

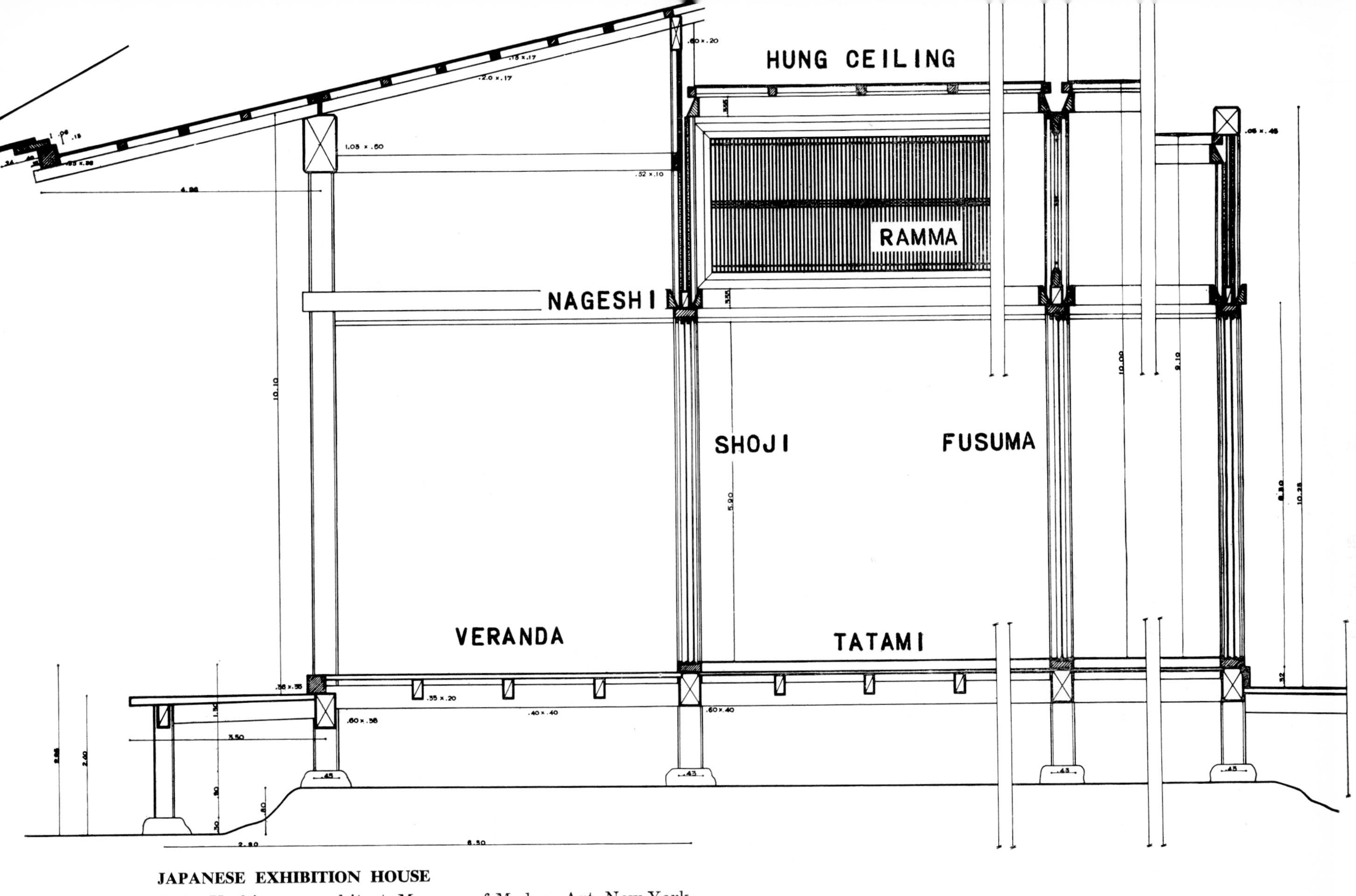

JAPANESE EXHIBITION HOUSE

Junzo Yoshimura, architect. Museum of Modern Art, New York.

Cross-section through the veranda (left) and main rooms (right) of a Japanese house, based on sixteenth-century prototypes.

THE IMPERIAL PALACE, KYOTO

The white plaster walls are divided by exposed horizontal bracing arranged with due regard for effects of scale. Wall and roof systems offer strong contrasts of linear and sculptural forms, heightened by the occasional omission of a wall. Covered verandas connecting these buildings were removed during World War II to prevent fire from spreading.

umns, thus preserving the continuity of structural delineation. But on walls meeting each other at a right angle the *nageshi* are often at slightly different heights—the difference being from one half to two or three times the depth of the *nageshi* itself. This abrupt denial of continuity focuses attention on the corner of a room, as if to accent the limits of the space it contains. And the consequent differences in the height of the *ramma* on adjoining walls has the further effect of forcing into prominence one wall otherwise no more important than the others. This seemingly disjunctive structural grammar provides an unfailingly effective emphasis in an architecture not susceptible to more drastic axial and hierarchic development.

Every aspect of its design suggests that a Japanese building is a kind of fable, elaborately shrouding such elements of the structure as do not lend themselves to a poetic rendition. Apart from all other details the ceiling of a Japanese house alone would justify this view. It is true that in farmhouses, and in temples and certain other large buildings that are almost entirely open in plan, the immensely complicated superstructures are often revealed. But urbane usage requires the quantities of space, so carefully delineated by columns, *tatami, nageshi* and *ramma,* to be completed by flat ceilings. The framing of the roof is not to be seen. What is seen instead is a pattern of very light wood strips rather like battens, placed perhaps 18 inches apart. These strips are fastened to a ledge on the wall, called *mawaribuchi,* and during construction are temporarily held aloft by a pole suspended from the rafters. The ⅛ inch thick boards which make the finished ceiling are placed on top of the strips so that they overlap each other, and are nailed to the strips from above. At intervals a somewhat heavier strip is nailed on top of the boards, and to this in turn are attached several wood poles which, finally, are nailed to the rafters far above. Other methods also produce hung ceilings of that esthetic simplicity for which the Japanese are justly famed.

At the intersection of wall and ceiling occurs what is called the *tenjo-nageshi.* It is often given the appearance of a major structural element, consonant with an architecture in which surfaces, including ceilings, are subordinate to lines. But the articulation of every element in the composition of a room produced effects antipathetic to each other. For example, it was felt that the *ramma,* particularly when it was a plaster panel, detracted from the *tenjo-nageshi* so that the ceiling itself seemed inadequately supported. This defect was remedied by inserting, just below the ceiling, a strip of white plaster wall perhaps 6 or 8 inches high. The extra band of plaster made the wood ceiling appear to float effort-

KATSURA IMPERIAL VILLA

The influence of tea house architecture in this formal reception room is revealed by the rounded corner post of the *tokonoma,* and by a round *nageshi* above the sliding screens.

lessly above the room, but at the same time the *tenjo-nageshi* was deprived of any apparent structural purpose. In reality, of course, it had no significant structural function, but in conformity with other such details it had always been articulated as an element of structure rather than decoration. Columns could not be allowed to interrupt the extra band of plaster even though the logic of the structure as a whole suggested that they should, because such an interruption would mean the loss of effects advantageous for the ceiling. Sought for their own right rather than to clarify the initial concept of a structural cage, such secondary effects were finally organized into a separate system. The unusual merit of this new style was its integration of acutely disparate ideas. Called *Sukiya-zukuri,* its development was brought about by the requirements of the tea ceremony, which included a special room and finally a separate house as part of its equipage. The *Sukiya* style produced minor masterpieces of an architecture difficult to understand without a detailed knowledge of the literary and metaphysical speculations which sustained it.

Another effect proper to Japanese architecture, but infrequently exploited, is the arrangement of the rooms in a building so that not all of them directly adjoin each other. Like boxes of varying sizes packed unevenly in a carton, rooms may be separated from each other by an unused, wasted space. In practice this ambiguous area may serve as a passageway or, perhaps, as in the example at Katsura Palace, as a dressing room. Considered as an esthetic device alone, the function of such an irregular space is to reveal the corners of the rooms adjoining it, thus making it possible to experience those rooms both from within and without as complete, independent volumes. Such an arrangement unexpectedly emphasizes Japanese architecture's underlying concept of additive, cellular space, even though it requires the introduction of a secondary space which, like an organ-point in musical composition, remains free of the harmonies it supports.

The limits of each room are given their most important definition not by the sliding screens but by the band of white plaster wall above them. Together with the ceiling this raised wall makes the upper part of a room a kind of lid floating just above eye level. When the sliding screens are opened to the view, it is the band of solid wall above which seems to keep the inhabitants of the room from falling out into the landscape. The proportions of the fixed upper wall may be readily adjusted to the requirements of a particular room by raising or lowering the ceiling height, since the ceilings of individual rooms are suspended from the roof beams and can be fixed at any appropriate level. The architect is thus enabled to maintain throughout the building one height for all sliding wall screens, without thereby sacrificing minute but necessary local variations in scale.

The relative absence of a monumental scale in classical Japanese architecture, and of forms appropriate to it, has often been attributed to geographical and climatic conditions. Heavy rainfall, abundant forests, and the constant threat of earthquakes are regarded as having made inevitable the intense refinement of wood architecture. Stone, however, is as readily available in Japan as timber, and the dangers of seismic disturbances are at best minimized rather than overcome by construction in wood. In fact it may be noted that earthquakes are most successfully defied by stone walls such as those found in the castles of Nagoya and Osaka. Nor is the monumental scale inaccessible to the Japanese spirit: Emperor Nintoku's burial mound covers 80 acres (the great pyramid at Gizeh occupies 13.1 acres); mural paintings like those of Kano Eitoku and his school are a sustained, powerful outpouring of color and massive pattern; and the *Noh* drama, with its stately evocation of the tragic spirit, has for the Japanese that resounding authority of insight which the Western world finds in Sophocles and Shakespeare.

Nevertheless, the Japanese sense of form does not reveal itself most clearly in monumental conceptions. Poetry, painting and music no less than architecture affirm instead a preoccupation with the refinement of form. But both the miniature and the monumental (with certain notorious exceptions) are subject to the same standards: restraint and sobriety, and, among other things, a mildly negative response to the temptations of worldly experience. All of these modes of feeling are themselves part of the Japanese conception of simplicity, which does not necessarily include the spontaneous and direct. Something astringent, restrained, and sober is *shibui,* the Japanese say, and reflects an austere taste informed with a certain pleasurable melancholy. Delighting in the transient and cultivating the accidental, *shibui* nevertheless is sustained by a furious energy, purposeful and unrelenting, and in its characteristic game of reconciling contradictions lies what may be the essence of the Japanese sensibility.

3

Ancient Korea had three major kingdoms. Two of them, Silla and Kokuli, made war on Paikche, their neighbor. In 552 envoys from the King of Paikche applied for military aid to the Emperor of Yamato, whose domains then comprised the western half of Honshu and a foothold on Korea itself. The envoys also delivered an image of the Buddha, with a message from the King of Paikche recommending the new doctrines as the best of all religions. The gift of Buddhism eventually altered and enriched every aspect of Japanese life, but at first it was identified with the interests of rival factions at the Imperial court. There it became the personal commitment of Soga-no-Umako, a Minister who set himself to importing everything necessary to the temporal organization of the new faith. It remained for the scholarly Prince Shotoku Taishi to import the moral and philosophical content, while balancing the interests of the ascendant Soga family against the conservative guardians of the native Shintoism. Monks and architects began to arrive from Paikche in 577. By 640 Buddhist temples in Japan numbered forty-six; by 697 there were over five hundred.

Horyuji Temple was founded in 607 by Empress Suiko. Its earliest surviving buildings reflect a style of architecture current in China perhaps one hundred years earlier, and indeed they constitute a record of building types now vanished from both China and Korea. One influence of the Korean kingdoms is found in Horyuji's Kondo, or main hall, which was built with the Korean foot measure prohibited in Japan after 645. Horyuji's full name is Horyu Gakumonji, which means Learning Temple, and it was in fact a combination of temple and college. The earlier Korean and Japanese plan for this complex of functions began with a large cloistered court approached from the south through the Nandaimon, the Great Southern Gate. On a north-south axis through the center of the site four structures were aligned: The Chumon, or middle gate; the pagoda; the Kondo; and the lecture hall, called Kodo. Buildings outside the enclosure on the north, east, and west housed the monks. At Horyuji this plan was modified. Within the cloistered court the Kondo and the pagoda are placed not on the central axis, where they can be seen only in sequence, but to the east and west of the axis, where their varied heights and proportions are seen in relation to each other and to the cloistered walk. The Kondo stands on a stone podium, and its round columns have a slight entasis, like their Chinese prototypes. The columns, which rest on flat stones, are surmounted with round plates carrying clusters of brackets to make possible a greater extension of the cantilevered roofs. Conforming with the equal prominence given to the main hall and the

HORYUJI TEMPLE

Inside the temple compound are the pagoda and the Kondo. Both buildings were destroyed by fire in 1949, and are now being reconstructed. The gatehouse, called Chumon, is at the far left; the lecture hall is at the right.

pagoda, the middle gate incorporates two entrances side by side, rather than one.

A pagoda either marks a sacred site or contains a Buddhist relic; in Japan it is most often used for the latter purpose, the relic being contained in a cup hollowed out of a stone. This stone is placed under the central shaft, which rises the entire height of the structure. The area at ground level is walled in, despite the fact that the enclosing *mokoshi,* or "skirt-building," mars the effect of weightlessness produced by the tiers of roofs above. Like the Kondo, Horyuji's five-storeyed pagoda stands on a stone platform, and it is balanced and partially supported by its single huge central column. Lesser columns surrounding this shaft support beams which in turn carry more columns, for each of the five cantilevered roofs.

Derived, through China, from the Indian Stupa, in which the universe and the axis on which it revolves are represented by a dome surmounted by a spire, the pagoda became a giant architectural ornament retaining, at its top, only a miniature replica of the forms from which it evolved. This evolution was influenced by construction in wood rather than stone, and a striking example of its technical refinement is provided by the pagoda of Yakushiji Temple. Founded around 680, Yakushiji was reproduced in Heijo, near modern Nara, when the capital was moved there at the beginning of the eighth century. Esthetically Yakushiji's pagoda is far more complex than Horyuji's. Each floor has two projecting roofs rather than one. The *mokoshi* seen at the ground floor of Horyuji pagoda is here repeated on each level, and at each level it is equipped with its own roof. The "real" roof above it, much larger, thus appears to be a pedestal for the next *mokoshi.* These skirt walls serve primarily to mask the cluttered structure from which the roofs are cantilevered. The total number of storeys is three, but the number of roofs suggests that there are six. And where Horyuji's pagoda relies for its effect on the diminishing size and the curvature of its roofs, Yakushiji's introduces alternately large and small roofs in a complicated rhythm at least as important as their curvature. Curiously animated, even restless, the roofs of Yakushiji pagoda, when seen from below, combine to hide the *mokoshi* walls and thus seem to be hanging in air like beads on an invisible string.

Yakushiji's pagoda is the surviving member of a two-part composition; originally it was adjoined on the west by another pagoda identical to it. Both of them were placed within the temple compound on either side of the north-south axis, recalling the earlier Korean style at Horyuji but being in fact a modification of another arrangement im-

HORYUJI TEMPLE

The Kondo and the pagoda are on either side of a north-south axis terminated by the gatehouse, in the background. Exposed structural framing of these buildings is painted red, with yellow accents.

PAGODA OF HORYUJI TEMPLE

All visible structural members for the roofs are cantilevered. Since the balconies are not accessible, their railings at each floor serve no practical purpose. The enclosure at the ground floor, called *mokoshi,* is believed to have been added about one hundred years after the pagoda was built. The reconstruction now in progress will include this wall, but the pagoda will first be photographed without it to provide a record of what its original appearance is assumed to have been.

PAGODA OF YAKUSHIJI TEMPLE

The *mokoshi* at ground floor level is repeated on each storey, and is equipped with its own roof. These smaller roofs appear to be pedestals for each of the three large roofs, and suggest that the pagoda has six rather than three storeys. Columns in the wall plane rest on cantilevered members and serve primarily to stiffen the thin plaster walls.

PAGODA OF YAKUSHIJI TEMPLE
Bracket arms reinforce the concealed, cantilevered roof beams.

ported from China. In effect the pagoda was demoted, having been taken off the central axis, as was done at Horyuji. But here the Kondo, or main hall, is assigned a dominant position on the axis, and as a result two pagodas were required to balance the design. Many of these developments were encouraged by the spirit of the Taikwa Reforms, inaugurated in 646 by the Minister Nakatomi-no-Kamatari, whose enthusiastic adaptations of T'ang dynasty productions extended to politics, economics, and religion as well as esthetics.

Technical dexterity of the kind that made possible the pagodas of Yakushiji and Horyuji also produced another kind of structure which, though unrelated in design or function, is not less intricately calculated. The most impressive example of this building type is the log treasure house in Nara, called the Shosoin. Stored in this box-like building, without benefit of lock and key, are invaluable documents, pictures, musical instruments, weapons, and utensils, as well as foreign glass and textiles. This treasure was deposited in the Shosoin by the widow of Emperor Shomu, in 756. Slips of paper signed by each succeeding Emperor, and attached to each of the building's three doors, have always been sufficient protection against intruders. Today the Shosoin is patrolled by a guard whose chief duty it is to sound the alarm in case of fire.

The Shosoin is built on a platform 108 feet long, held 9 feet above the ground by forty massive columns. Log walls divide the platform into three compartments. All the logs are triangular in cross-section; intersecting and overlapping at the corners of each compartment, they present a faceted surface to the weather side while forming a perfectly smooth interior wall. In hot dry weather the logs shrink away from each other and allow fresh air to circulate within, but during wet weather they expand and seal the building, thus keeping the interior dry. The whole structure is covered by a single tile roof, its weight being transmitted to the columns through the log walls. In this respect the Shosoin is a building type unique in the architecture of Japan, since the roof is carried by walls, rather than by isolated columns, and is necessarily the last part to be built.

Most heavily forested cold areas have produced a type of building in which thick log walls, sometimes with a caulking of mud, protect the inhabitants from severe cold. In Japan this type of construction is called *Azekura;* the Shosoin and many smaller storehouses similar to it are representative examples, but it is not quite clear why this construction was pursued for a while by a people otherwise so wholeheartedly devoted, despite the rigors of winter, to a light, open architecture. A more refined version of the *Azekura* style makes use of plank walls 2 inches thick, as in the treasure houses at Ise Shrine, but the general development of *Azekura* buildings seems influenced less by the availability of heavy timber, or by climate, than by the need for an architectural symbol of security to discourage intruders. Certainly the Shosoin itself is intended to be difficult of access: there are no stairs. Once a year, when the treasures are examined and ceremonially aired, a veranda and stairs are built along the front. The most important objects are removed from the building, set out on the lawn, inspected, and quickly returned to their places. The veranda with its stair is then dismantled.

To structural complexity and a certain devious practicality must be added another facet of Japan's classical architecture: great size. The largest wood building in the world under one roof is the Daibutsuden, the Hall of the Great Buddha, of Todaiji Temple, the Great Eastern Monastery of Nara. First built in 751 in an eastern quarter of the capital city, the Daibutsuden was destroyed by fire and rebuilt in the twelfth century. Eleven bays long from east to west and seven bays wide from north to south, the building originally measured 290 feet by 170 feet, and was 163 feet high, including the 11 foot stone base. In 1567 it again was burned, and after years of neglect was rebuilt, between 1696 and 1708, at two-thirds its original size. The Daibutsuden is now 188 feet in length, 166 feet in width, and 157 feet in height.

The Daibutsuden houses in a dim light a gilded bronze image of the Vairocana Buddha, twice partially destroyed by fire. Under the direction of a Korean expert the 53 foot high statue was cast in forty-odd stages, the head and neck being cast together as a separate shell 12 feet high. The discovery of a native source of gold by a provincial governor of the Junior Fifth Rank enabled its costly gilding to be completed. Even the original building, it may be conjectured, was not large enough to have accommodated comfortably so imposing a sculpture. Now, the statue seems to be wearing its building like a tight-fitting overcoat, leaving only cramped folds of space in which visitors struggle for a distorted view of the blackened, imperfect colossus.

The new state religion was shaped by six major sects, and three of them are of particular interest for their effect on Japan's art and thought. The Sanron sect, based on a Chinese version of a work by Nagarjuna, held that all phenomena are unreal and exist only relatively to one another. The Hosso sect was based on the commentaries of Vasubandhu, who asserted that the only reality is consciousness. The Hosso sect gained considerable power and eventually controlled its own temples, including Horyuji, which is today its headquarters. These and other sects were concerned pri-

THE SHOSOIN

The triangular logs of the Shosoin, an Imperial treasure house, produce a faceted exterior and a smooth interior wall. In wet weather the logs expand and seal the building; in dry weather they shrink and allow air to circulate within. Forty columns, deliberately split and bound with iron rings, hold the building 9 feet above the ground.

TODAIJI TEMPLE

Visitors pause at this pavilion to wash their hands in symbolic purification before entering the Daibutsuden.

DAIBUTSUDEN, TODAIJI TEMPLE

The figures in the pavilion, at the lower right, help to indicate the scale of Todaiji's Daibutsuden, the largest wood building in the world. The lower roof is cantilevered almost thirty feet. Columns and other structural details are painted red and yellow, and the tile ornaments on the ridge, representing the tail of a mythical bird, are covered with gold leaf.

marily with attaining salvation by ridding the mind of "sensory illusions," and were often expounded simultaneously in one monastery with the same interest later given by the Japanese to Christianity. In 733 two Japanese monks travelling in China invited to their homeland a renowned exponent of a disciplinary sect, the priest Ganjin. The adherents of this sect placed their hope for salvation in the orthodox observance of Buddhist ritual. After great hardships Ganjin reached Nara in 754, when he was sixty-seven years old, and blind. He was lodged in Todaiji, which was in effect the official seat of Buddhism, and he received from Emperor Shomu authority to perform the rites of ordination. A *kaidan,* the altar of ordination symbolized by a large high platform, was built at Todaiji and over four hundred persons, led by the Empress dowager, were received into the order. In the last years of his life Ganjin presided over Japan's central *kaidan,* transferred from Todaiji to a new temple built on a site given him by Emperor Shomu. The finest surviving example of Buddhist architecture in the T'ang dynasty style imported from China, during the Nara age, is the main hall of this temple, Toshodaiji, where Ganjin died.

Toshodaiji was built in 759. Its Kondo, the main or "golden" hall, houses a statue of the Vairocana Buddha and two attendant deities. This building is seven bays long and four bays deep, but the bays are of different sizes. The widest of them, at the center, is flanked by progressively diminishing bay widths, and the line of bays on the front and rear elevations are less deep than those inside the building. On the main elevation this rhythmic division of spaces was emphasized by setting the wall plane back on the second line of columns, thus creating a colonnade. The columns also have a slight entasis, and because they stand free of the wall they lend to the building a pronounced frontality seldom found in Japanese architecture unless it be of continental origin. Inside the building the altar is placed against a screen wall, rather than in the center of the hall, partially as a result of the spatially complex arrangement of bays.

Later refinements of technique allowed the true roof structure to be entirely concealed, including the lever arms which carry the eaves far beyond the exterior walls. But in its earlier phases the required cantilever could be made structurally secure only with the aid of an elaborate system of supporting brackets. These brackets, in their simplest form, occur as arms springing from either side of the column to shorten the span of beams in the wall plane. Later a beam at right angles to the wall plane was projected beyond the column, and on this, parallel with the wall, another member

KONDO, TOSHODAIJI TEMPLE

OVERLEAF:
Left: The colonnade of Toshodaiji's Kondo. The columns have a slight entasis, and the bay widths diminish at each end of the building. The wire screen to protect the bracket arms is a contemporary addition. In the background can be seen a small log treasure house of *Azekura* construction.
Right: The two central aisles of the building are treated as one hall, with a coffered and coved ceiling. Additional rooms are behind the statues of the Buddha and his attendants.

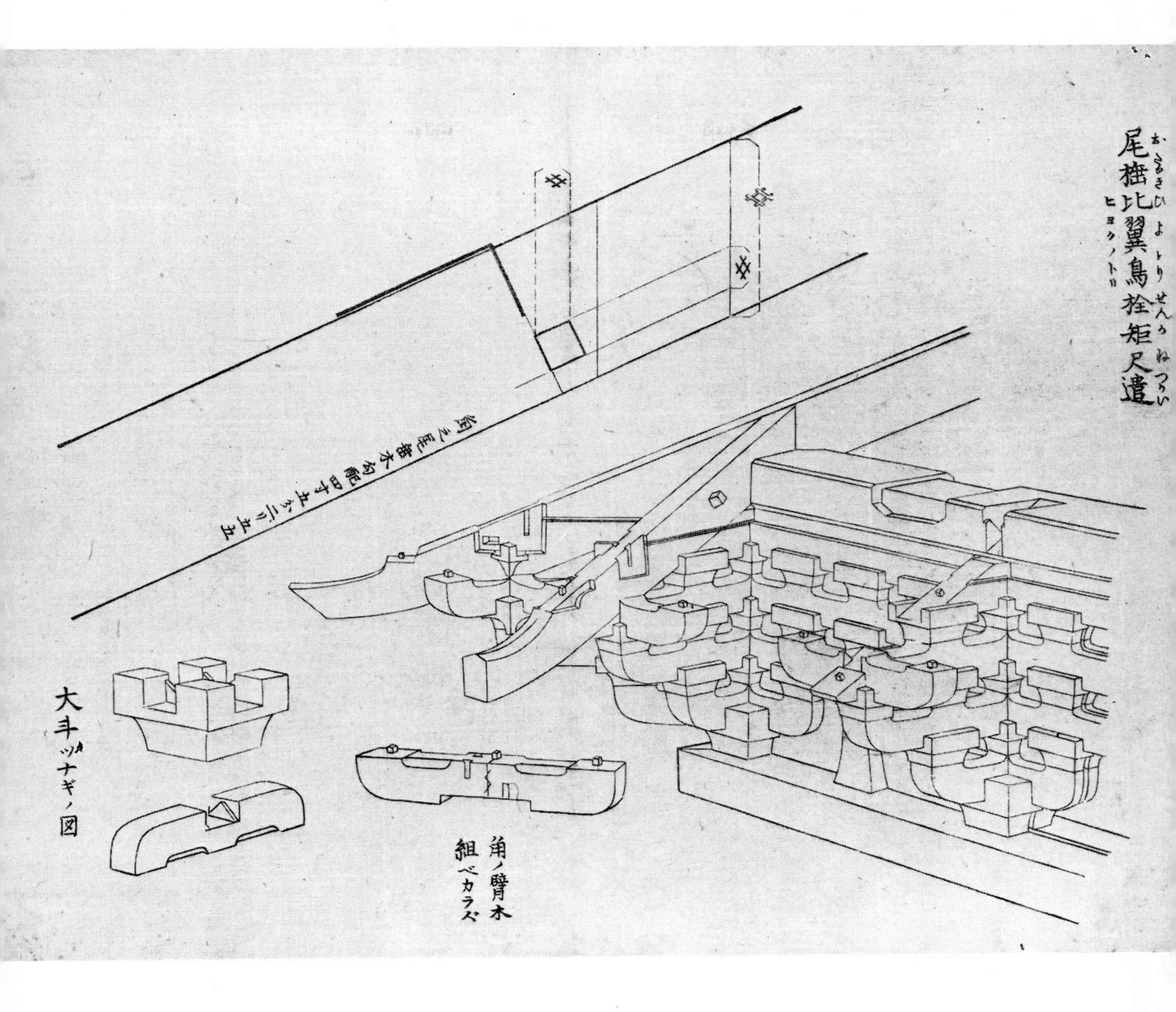

The component parts of a bracket system, in this drawing from an eighteenth-century carpenters' manual, are shown individually and assembled at the corner of a building. The short section of a rafter serves no structural purpose and is used only to fill out the pattern made by the real rafters, which are not shown in the drawing.

NINNAJI TEMPLE

The column and beams (above) and the carved capitals supporting bracket arms were photographed during the dismantling and reconstruction of the gate at Ninnaji Temple in 1937.

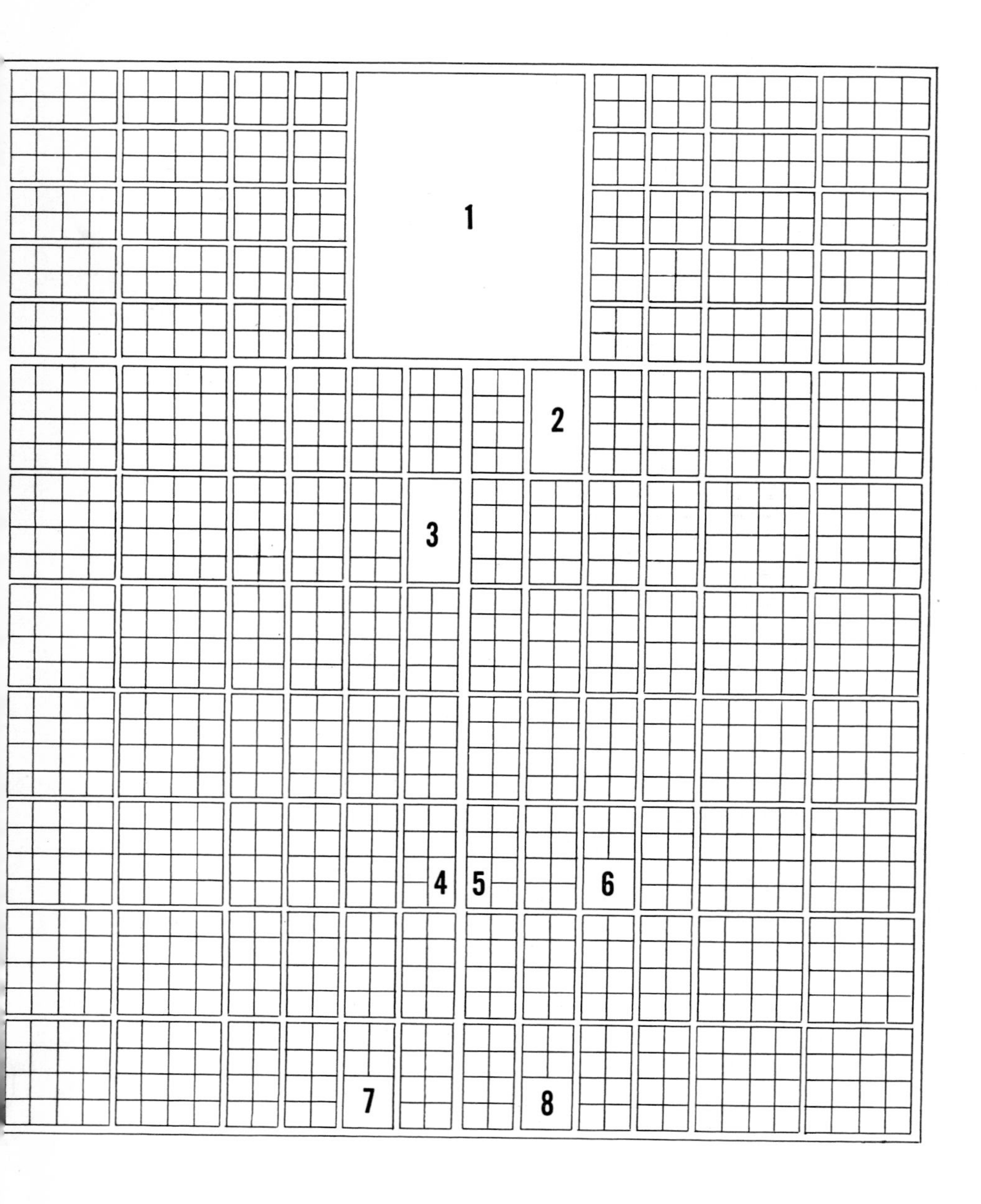

HEIAN-KYO

The eighth century gridiron plan for Heian-kyo was modeled on Chinese predecessors.

1	Imperial City
2, 3	Imperial Park and university buildings
4	West reception buildings
5	East reception buildings
6	East market
7	West temple
8	East temple

was placed to carry the purlin which supports the rafters. This arrangement takes the point of support one step out from the wall plane, but further developments multiply both the tiers of bracket arms and the number of steps away from the wall plane, until the purlins appear to be carried on a filigree of sculptured and sometimes painted ornament. It is believed that the Kondo's roof was made steeper in alterations during the seventeenth and nineteenth centuries. By that time the bracketing had been deprived of its original function, the true structure being concealed, and the roof of the Kondo illustrates certain ambiguities in the relation of the eaves line to the complicated but now decorative bracketing.

Death, in the ancient Japanese ontology, was associated with defilement. On the death of an Emperor it was customary to move the capital to a new site, which meant removing the palace buildings only a few miles or even hundreds of yards; the capital city itself probably remained unchanged. But by the Nara period architecture had become more substantial, and it was no simple thing to rebuild or move even the palace alone. Nevertheless, ceremonial defilement, the new power of the priesthood, and the political intrigues of the Fujiwara family seem to have prompted Emperor Kammu to build a new capital when he ascended the throne, and so in 782 the Nara period came to a close. Work began in 784 on a site at Nagaoka, and within five months the Emperor took up residence in the new palace. Construction of government buildings proceeded at great expense during the next ten years. Then, suddenly, an Imperial edict announced that the capital would be moved again. Ill-fortune, and the death of a trusted administrator in still another political intrigue, seem to have provoked Emperor Kammu's search for a more auspicious site. With the aid of diviners a site was selected about five miles from Nagaoka. It was named Heian-kyo, "the capital of peace and tranquility," and remained the capital of Japan until, in 1870, Edo became the Imperial Residence and was called Tokyo, or Eastern Capital. Heian-kyo was then distinguished from it by being called Kyoto, as it is known today.

Like Nara before it, the city of Heian was modeled on China's Sui dynasty capital at Ch'ang-an. Heian-kyo was a rectangle three and a half miles long from north to south and three miles wide from east to west. Situated on a flat, gently sloping plain near the Katsura river, it was enclosed by mist-shrouded mountains on the north, east, and west. Six streams were made to enter the city in canals, some of them wide enough for boats, and an embankment and a moat surrounded the entire rectangle. The city was divided into east and west districts by a great highway 250 feet wide, called the Shujaku. Entrance to this highway from the south was through a seven-portaled Great Gate, the Rashomon, and from there the road proceeded in a straight line to the southern gate of the Imperial Palace precincts at the northernmost end of the city. Paralleling the Shujaku were eight avenues 80 or 120 feet wide. Except for the 170 foot wide Nijo road fronting the Imperial enclosure, the east-west avenues were 80, 100, or 120 feet wide. The city unit, called a *cho,* was a block 400 feet square usually divided into thirty-two residential areas 50 by 100 feet. Smaller streets between *cho* were 40 feet wide, and all were bordered with moats and planted with willow and cherry trees.

Since many of the buildings were hidden from the streets by walls, the architectural character of the city was predominantly horizontal. But when seen from the mountains nearby the city's checkerboard pattern revealed the artfulness, somewhat removed from what really could be experienced down in the streets, with which an Imperial Park, a university, markets, and temples had been disposed within the grid. Like the fixed structural skeleton of a Japanese building, in which walls are merely shifting incidents, Heian-kyo's fixed grid of streets were not designed to lead from one building to another; the buildings, rather, were incidents fitted into the space between streets. The only interruption of the regular grid pattern was that made by the Imperial City enclosure at the north. There the Emperor presided, physically and symbolically, over a people ranged at his feet in living spaces commensurate with their place in the social structure of his "family." The size of a house was fixed by law, according to the rank of its owner. The highest possible rank, the Emperor's, required not a house but a city unto itself, a walled Imperial domain.

Completed by 804, the palace enclosure measures 1266 yards from east to west and 1533 yards from north to south, and originally contained about fifty buildings, including government offices, guardhouses, residences, temples, and, for the Imperial entertainment, a "Hall of Rich Pleasures." But perhaps the most notable of the original structures in the pure Chinese style was the Great Hall of State called the Daigokuden. This building was 170 feet long by 50 feet wide. Standing on a stone base, it was painted red and covered by a roof of blue tiles. It was not rebuilt after fire destroyed it in 1277. Of the buildings remaining today, as reconstructions, the most beautiful are the Shishinden and the Seiryoden. The Shishinden is the main reception hall of the palace, and it was to this building that the ceremony of accession to the throne was transferred after the destruction of the

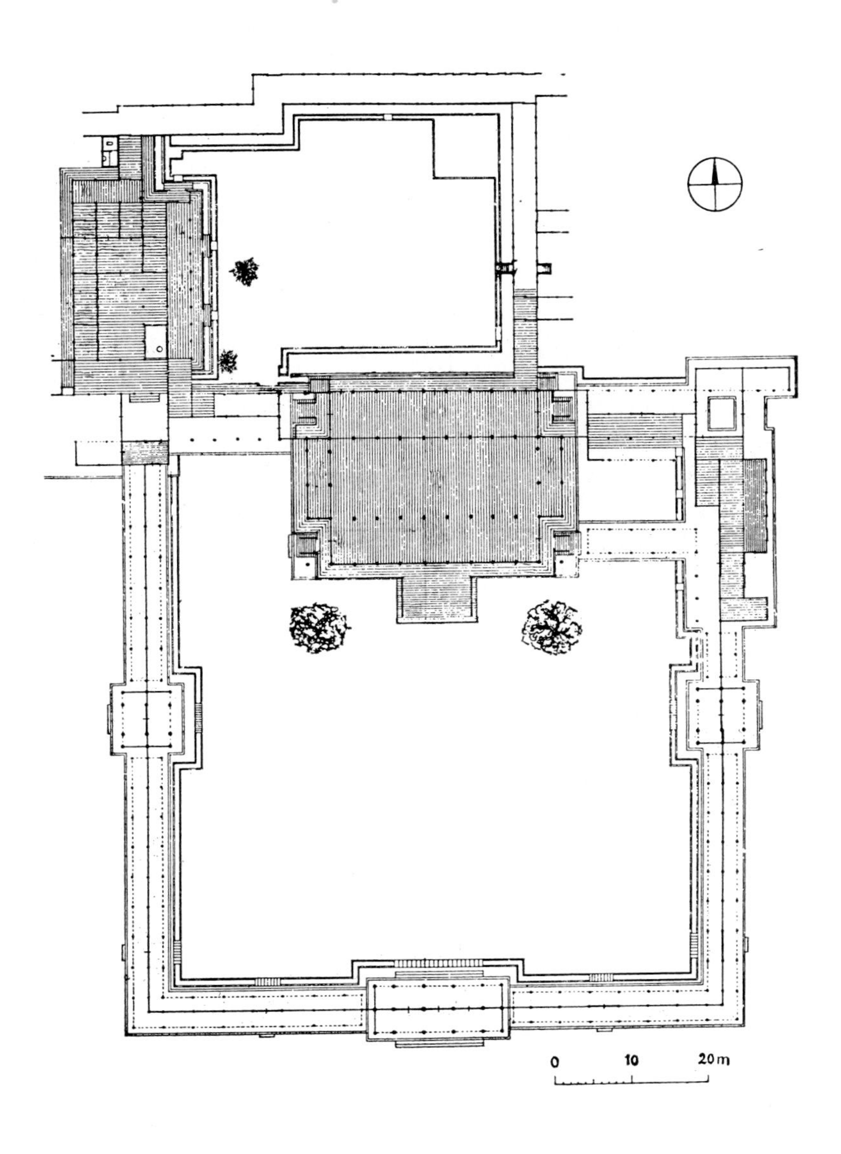

THE IMPERIAL PALACE, HEIAN-KYO (KYOTO)

Plan. Private apartments of the Emperor in the Seiryoden (upper left) are connected to the Enthronement Hall, called Shishinden, by covered galleries which also enclose the gardens.

Seiryoden

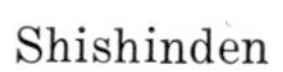

Shishinden

THE IMPERIAL PALACE, HEIAN-KYO (KYOTO)

Great Hall of State. The Seiryoden contains what were originally the private living quarters of Emperor Kammu.

The Shishinden is a spacious hall from which project, on each elevation, galleries called *hisashi-no-ma* (chambers under the eaves). In plan the building thus forms a cross, measuring 90 feet from east to west and 75 feet from north to south. At the front of the building, which faces south, a flight of eighteen broad steps leads to the veranda, and additional stairs are found at the corners of the building in the angle formed by the projecting galleries. The single *Irimoya* roof extends to cover these stairs, so that the whole structure appears to be a simple rectangular block the corner bays of which have been omitted. Although the roofs of the palace buildings retain the concave surfaces of their Chinese prototypes, they are nevertheless peculiarly Japanese in that all curves have been subdued. Only at the corners of the Shishinden do the eaves lift, very gently.

The south and east *hisashi-no-ma* open directly into the main hall; the north and west "chambers under the eaves" are closed from it by partition walls of sliding screens, this being one of the earliest uses of *fusuma*. The north wall is decorated with paintings in color of Chinese sages. Throughout the building the floor is of thick planks polished to a watery smoothness, reflecting the massive round columns. Neither the hall nor the galleries are ceiled, the dressed rafters being completely exposed, and no color is applied to the wood. In the center of the main hall stands the lacquered, lavishly decorated and canopied Imperial Throne. The extraordinary garden towards which the Shishinden opens is devoid of all planting except for an orange tree and a cherry tree, each enclosed in a bamboo fence; the rest of the garden is entirely surfaced with white sand raked in a pattern of straight lines. A high wall with three gates encloses the area, the tile roof of this wall being carried out beyond it to form a cloister-like walk around the great expanse of sand. Only on ceremonial occasions are the gates opened and the garden used.

Contrasting with the polished grandeur of the Shishinden is the elegant intricacy of the Emperor's private apartments, the Seiryoden. Facing east to another sand garden, smaller than that which fronts the Enthronement Hall, the Seiryoden comprises a main chamber which serves as a living room, flanked on the north by a dining room, bed chamber, bath and dressing rooms, and apartments for the Imperial consorts. Kitchen and storage quarters are on the west. Rooms for the servants and apartments for the court were in separate buildings reached by covered galleries. Measuring 60 feet long by 30 feet wide, the Seiryoden is raised above the

SHISHINDEN, THE IMPERIAL PALACE

Steps to the southern veranda are made of thick planks in single lengths. The ends of each plank are painted white as a protection against the effects of weathering; originally white paper was pasted to the wood for this purpose.

SHISHINDEN, THE IMPERIAL PALACE

The sand garden of the Shishinden, used only on ceremonial occasions is enclosed on three sides by a covered gallery. Columns and wood doors of the gallery are painted red. An orange tree (left) and a cherry tree on the other side of the stairs are the garden's only ornaments.

SHISHINDEN, THE IMPERIAL PALACE

Galleries inside the Shishinden, called *hisashi-no-ma,* (galleries under the eaves) open directly into the main hall but can be closed to the veranda by hinged wall panels called *shitomido*. These panels are held aloft by iron rods suspended from the ceiling. Protection from the sun is afforded by finely woven bamboo blinds called *sudari,* which are shown partially unrolled.

The Imperial Throne (right) stands on a lacquered dais and is covered by a silk canopy. Exposed beams here and in the outer galleries are unpainted but precisely finished. The Shishinden is still used for the enthronement ceremony.

SEIRYODEN, THE IMPERIAL PALACE

At one end of the suite built for Emperor Kammu is a floor made of waxed white plaster. The observance of certain religious ceremonies required the Emperor to be in contact with the earth, which in inclement weather is represented by the plaster floor. The metal lid covers a sunken charcoal brazier.

SEIRYODEN, THE IMPERIAL PALACE

Exposed structural framing of the buildings which enclose the Seiryoden's garden provide a pattern of carefully composed rectangles. The value attached to such patterns can be gauged by the fact that these walls are the only view from the Emperor's private apartments.

Hinged wall panels (left) are made of thin sheets of wood reinforced on both sides by wood strips. The rolled bamboo blind bound with silk tape can be seen, in relation to the columns, in the photograph on page 106.

OVERLEAF:
Gallery connecting the Seiryoden and the Shishinden. The narrow section is removed during a yearly ceremony, when a messenger on horseback rides out of the enclosure bearing the Emperor's written greetings to the deity at Ise Shrine.

ground and surrounded by a veranda reached from the sand garden by two short flights of steps. Here again are two trees only—this time clumps of bamboo on either side of the south stair. Originally water flowed here in several streams bordered with bamboo groves, but in the tenth century the garden was modified to its present austere state. It is enclosed on the south by the rear elevation of the Shishinden, and on the east and north by the galleries and offices which connect both the Shishinden and the Seiryoden with other parts of the palace precincts. Bordering all the buildings around the court is a narrow stone trench to carry off rainwater shed by the overhanging eaves. Emphatically incised into the earth, this stone trench is a sharp line of demarcation between buildings and garden no less effective than a podium. No effort is made, as in later Japanese architecture, to relate a building to its garden by stepping-stones or planting. Instead the composition depends on the grouping of buildings so that they block, and at the same time create, courtyards of different sizes; the Seiryoden, for example, is virtually a platform placed to close off a kind of outdoor alcove formed by the almost blank rear walls of three different buildings.

The walls of these connecting buildings are of white plaster, divided by their wood structural framework into compositions of thoughtfully related rectangles. The cool facades which thus constitute the only view from the Emperor's apartments are a study in abstract pattern, free of sculpture or other ornament. Like the accidentally textured and shadowed walls admired by Leonardo da Vinci for the images they suggested, these walls can also be "read," but only for deliberate harmonies of proportion.

Outside Heian-kyo the Imperial edicts concerning frugality, as manifested in the size of an aristocrat's country house, were more difficult to impose. One reason was that the Emperors, forced to live in the country mansions of their regents during occasions of political and military stress, eventually undertook to build country palaces of their own. Partly through the example of Chinese predecessors, the mansions of the Fujiwara regents, and the Shishinden of the Imperial Palace itself, there developed late in the Heian period (898-1185) a type of country residence consisting of semi-detached buildings grouped around a large reception room called *shinden*. This room was also used as a bed chamber and so was roofed with thatch, on which rain makes little noise. The *shinden* faced south to a wide lake (usually artificial) and was flanked west and east by covered galleries leading to pavilions for, respectively, fishing and enjoying the cool breeze. The lake sometimes flowed under part of the

ITSUKUSHIMA SHRINE
The buildings are of formal *shinden* design developed under the Fujiwara regents. Columns and some structural details, painted red, reveal Chinese influence.

shinden and the east and west pavilions, and bridges led from the garden "mainland" to a diminutive island in the "sea." Entrance to the estate was through gates in the covered galleries. North of the main buildings were additional houses for the women and the family, all connected by the rambling covered corridors. At first the plan was symmetrical, but in time the arrangement was varied according to the exigencies of the site and a preference for more unexpected groupings. Called *Shinden-zukuri* (the *Shinden* way of building), these estates appear in scroll paintings of the time to illustrate the dwelling arrangements Buddhists anticipated in paradise.

While the Emperor officiated at certain religious ceremonies, poetry composing contests, or excursions to view the moon, the country during the Heian age was actually under the control of Fujiwara regents only technically appointed by the court. For a time the Fujiwara balanced opposing factions by paying them off with tax-free estates and honorary titles, but eventually the lords in the provinces, grown wealthy, were able to defy not only Imperial pronouncements but the control of the Fujiwara as well. By 1185 Minamoto Yoritomo, having overthrown the Fujiwara, extracted from the Emperor an edict making him Shogun, or commander-in-chief. Yoritomo set up an army headquarters called the Bakufu in Kamakura, which place then became the real capital even though the Emperor continued to live at Heian-kyo. The military vassals of the Minamoto and other clans had by now achieved a new status. Called *samurai,* these knights formed a powerful class with an austere code of ethics exalting military hardship and devotion to their leaders. *Samurai* houses by the end of the Kamakura period differed from the Heian aristocracy's *Shinden* mansions primarily in that most of the rooms were under one roof; galleries connecting separate wings do not seem to have been used. Possibly this more compact plan was developed for security, since *samurai* houses were often surrounded by board fences and, sometimes, there were towers for archers. Sliding doors of wood and of paper seem generally to have replaced the hinged, two-part horizontal wood doors of *Shinden* palaces. The floors were of wood, with cushions placed only where needed. In such a house one room was equipped with a built-in desk called a *shoin;* this new architectural feature was introduced through Zen Buddhism, recently arrived from China. The *samurai* found in Zen doctrines much that was in sympathy with their own strenuous code, but since the Kamakura government had to import from the effete Heian capital officials who could read and write, *samurai* adaptations of Zen library desks must have been primarily an expression of respect or religious enthusiasm. The room with a desk was likely to be the finest in the house: guests were received in it. In time it was called simply the *shoin* room, and eventually the term *Shoin-zukuri* designated *samurai* dwellings in distinction to the *Shinden-zukuri* mansions of the Heian aristocracy. Often the *shoin* was on a dais in one corner of the room. Behind the *shoin* itself were small sliding *shoji* to admit light, and on the adjoining wall was an alcove called a *tokonoma,* in which were displayed such works of art as a scroll of calligraphy, a painting, or a beautiful vase. The *tokonoma* was also an adaptation of a Zen idea: a Zen Buddhist shrine was at first a small table holding a candle, flowers, and a censer, but eventually it was incorporated into the architecture as a shallow alcove raised one step above the floor. Similarly, a cabinet with shelves used in *Shinden* mansions developed into the *chigai-dana,* a niche built into the wall near the *shoin,* for storing papers and small objects.

When Kamakura rule was overthrown by the Ashikaga, the capital was re-established at Heian-kyo. Eight successive Ashikaga Shoguns gave the arts precedence over affairs of state; Japan is now rich in Chinese art of the Sung, Yuan, and Ming periods as a particular result of Ashikaga Yoshimasa's dalliance. The tea ceremony, an outgrowth of a Zen practice, was the special enthusiasm of Yoshimasa, who with the advice and assistance of the monk-artist Noami codified the Japanese taste for the austere and evocative. The last of the Ashikaga Shoguns lived in mansions of elegant *Shoin* design. Board floors were used but straw mats *(tatami)* were placed freely around the rooms. Black and white paintings on the sliding paper walls and in the *tokonoma* were the only decoration, and sometimes the columns were lacquered black. Landscape paintings and drawings in black ink are perhaps the most enduring monument to the dry, sometimes melancholy Ashikaga taste.

By 1467 the Ashikaga lost political control. Civil war began and presently embroiled the whole of Japan. From 1500 to 1600 the struggle for the redistribution of feudal power continued. During this time the foundations of modern Japan were established by three extraordinary men: Oda Nobunaga, who subjugated contending factions and succeeded in becoming the *de facto* Shogun; Toyotomi Hideyoshi, a soldier who rose from the ranks to become a general of Nobunaga's armies and ruler of Japan; and Tokugawa Ieyasu, an aristocrat who joined forces first with Nobunaga and then with Hideyoshi. As regent, Hideyoshi continued Nobunaga's subjugation of provincial lords with such success that he found time to launch a futile attack on China,

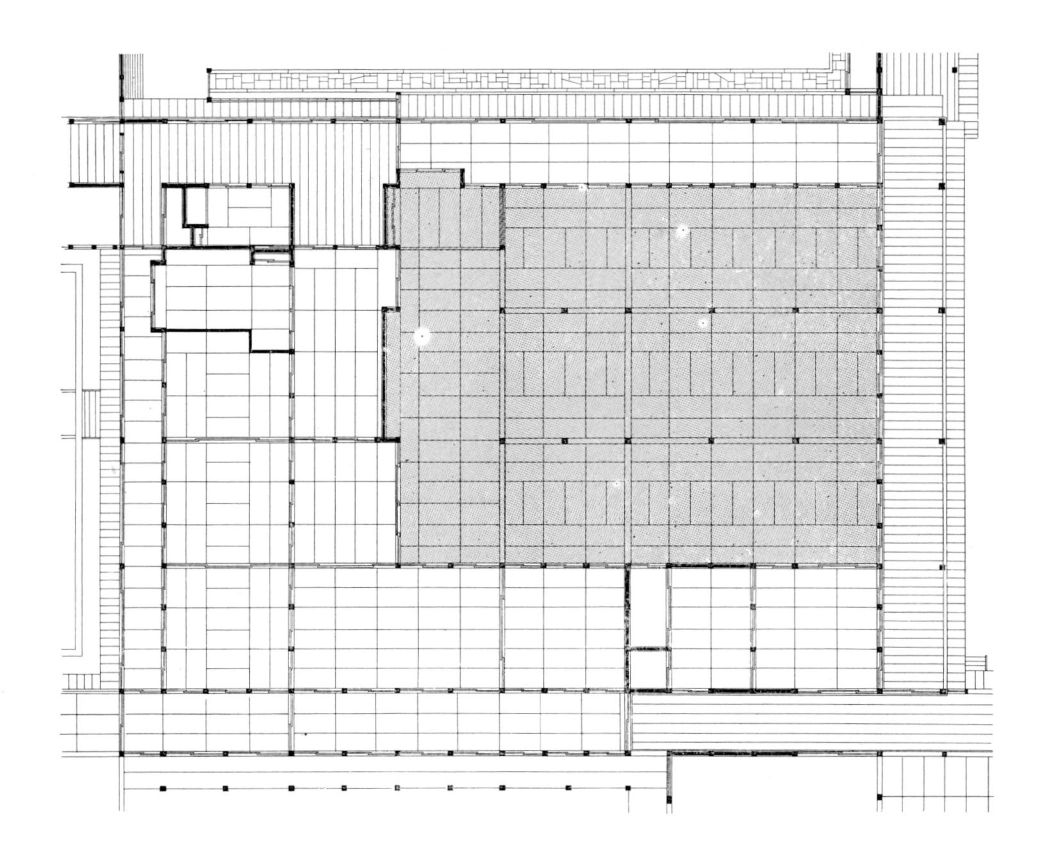

AUDIENCE HALL, NISHI-HONGANJI TEMPLE

Plan. The Great Hall of Audience (shaded gray) includes a dais called a *jodan,* at the left, and opens to a veranda and a courtyard on the right. The Hall is adjoined by dressing rooms and, behind the *jodan,* rooms for Hideyoshi's armed guard.

AUDIENCE HALL, NISHI-HONGANJI TEMPLE

The *ramma* between the Hall proper and the *jodan* are wood carvings of wild geese, reeds, and clouds. The framework of the suspended coffered ceiling is lacquered black and decorated with gold fittings, and the coffers are lacquered red, green, black, and gold. Black-lacquered floor plates between columns, set flush with the *tatami,* reflect the dark brown unpainted columns. The *tatami* are identical in color and texture but those in the center, arranged to form a path the length of the Hall, catch the light at a different angle and appear darker.

through Korea, before his death in 1598. Ieyasu, appointed Shogun, completed the political reorganization begun by his predecessors and made the Tokugawa family supreme in Japan for two hundred and fifty years.

A contributing factor to the civil wars had been armed bands of Buddhist monks. Threatening violence unless they received new tax-free lands, and other considerations of a metaphysical nature, they descended on Heian-kyo and fought in its streets. Buddhist temples thus incurred Nobunaga's special enmity, and Nobunaga burned what he disliked. Hideyoshi, more thoughtful, found other methods of exerting control, and the age was great not for its temple architecture but for its palaces and castles. Under Hideyoshi's lavish patronage the arts burst into new and colorful play. Given to entertainments on the grand scale, Hideyoshi did not hesitate to remodel and enlarge a temple to accommodate his three thousand guests, and in his castles at Momoyama (from which the age takes its name) and at Osaka the walls all but dissolved in a polychromy of gold-ground paintings, red and black lacquer and gold hardware. Extravagant, even boisterous, as Hideyoshi was he nevertheless paid more than homage to the Heian capital's stern canons of elegance, as set forth by the Ashikaga Shoguns. Advised by the tea master Sen-no-Rikyu, as Yoshimasa was advised by Noami, Hideyoshi also sought and encouraged a parallel art of intense refinement.

The Great Hall of Audience in Kyoto's Nishi-Honganji Temple was first built in 1594 as a reception room in Hideyoshi's Fushimi-Momoyama castle. In 1632 Ieyasu transferred the Hall and a garden designed for it to Nishi-Honganji. Based on a *ken* module of 7½ feet, the Hall proper is a chamber approximately 15 feet high and 67 feet square, open at the west to a platform one shallow step above it. On this platform, called the *jodan,* Hideyoshi sat to receive his vassals. The *jodan* runs the entire width of the room except for a portion at the right raised one more step. This smaller dais is equipped with a *shoin* and a *chigai-dana,* and is screened from the Hall by a partition pierced with a round window. On the rear wall of the *jodan* is a *tokonoma* 18 feet wide. To the left of it are heavily framed *fusuma* decorated with paintings on a gold ground. (Behind these *fusuma* an armed guard waited on the alert.) Rows of columns divide the Hall into three galleries, the central one being demarcated from the others by plaster panels between the columns, just under the ceiling. Bilateral symmetry is used here to focus attention on the *jodan:* like a nave flanked by side aisles the central gallery establishes an axis, reinforced by the plaster panels above, and reiterated below by strips of

Hideyoshi's seat on the *jodan,* from which he addressed his vassals, is made of two thick *tatami.* The paintings are attributed to Kano Tannyu.

AUDIENCE HALL, NISHI-HONGANJI TEMPLE

A distortion in column spacing is visible from the side aisles of the Hall, looking toward the *jodan*. The last two bays are ½ *ken* smaller than the others, which makes the room appear longer than it actually is.

black-lacquered wood set into the floor between the columns. Such floor plates are required when columns occur in the middle of a room because the mats can not conveniently be notched to fit around the columns, and the gap that remains in at least one direction is filled by a wood insert. In the Audience Hall this practical necessity has been exploited for reasons of esthetics.

On the north, east, and south walls columns are spaced on a 1 *ken* module, but columns in the center of the room, for the first three bays on the east, are set 2 *ken* apart. The last two bays, on the west, are each 1½ *ken* wide, the change in rhythm being marked on the floor by another strip of black lacquer running parallel with the *jodan*. Some columns on the north and south walls fail to correspond in placement with the columns at the west end of the central gallery, but this may not have been noticed by Hideyoshi's audience when, facing him, they enjoyed one of the rare examples in Japanese architecture of a perspective artificially lengthened, in this case by a reduction of the space between columns at one end of the room so that to the eye the total distance seems greater than it actually is. On the north the Hall is bounded by a closed corridor which can be opened to the garden, but on the east it opens directly to a veranda and a courtyard, in which stands a stage for the *Noh* drama.

In the fourteenth century native and imported ritual dances and entertainments were given a coherent dramatic form by two men: Kanami, a Shinto priest whose narrative dances relating the histories of temples were favored by the Shogun Ashikaga Yoshimitsu, and Kanami's son, Seami, a gifted actor, playwright, and producer. For Seami beauty consisted of realism: the imitation of nature. But by imitation Seami meant the abstract representation of life through gesture and sound. A gesture too closely reproducing a real act was, and is today, regarded as cheap trickery. By Western standards the *Noh* drama lacks development of plot or character, and conflicts seem arbitrarily terminated rather than resolved. But Seami's aim was to recreate in his audience an acute experience of what the national temperament regards as beautiful, dwelling on the poignancy of an emotion rather than on its origin or its outcome. Real and supernatural persons and events are represented, albeit abstractly, like the poor and humble fisherman whose goodness is revealed by his white kimono.

As the dramatis personae are abstractions of people and supernatural beings, so the *Noh* stage itself is an abstraction of Japanese architecture. Set in a sand-strewn courtyard (a purified landscape) it is a platform 18 feet square (a single pure unit of space) with a column at each corner supporting,

NOH STAGE, NISHI-HONGANJI TEMPLE

A stage for the performance of the *Noh* drama stands in the court-yard adjoining Hideyoshi's Audience Hall. Covered by a gable roof of *hinoki* bark, the stage proper is 18 feet square. The gallery at the left leads to a dressing room in a separate building. Spectators sat in the sand-strewn courtyard or on the veranda of the Audience Hall.

Actors, musicians, and chorus on a *Noh* stage.

STAGE DIRECTIONS FOR NOH DRAMA

The diagram and accompanying text from a program book contain instructions for speed of walking, gestures, and some of the dialogue in one short scene from a *Noh* drama. The sequence begins with the actor standing at the spot marked by a white dot, and ends at the white circle. Among the instructions noted are ". . . when 'cherry tree blossom' is spoken point toward left with right hand, then take one step toward left . . .", etc. In its almost choreographic concern with patterns of movement the *Noh* drama parallels Japanese garden design, in which movements are often regulated by the texture and spacing of stepping stones.

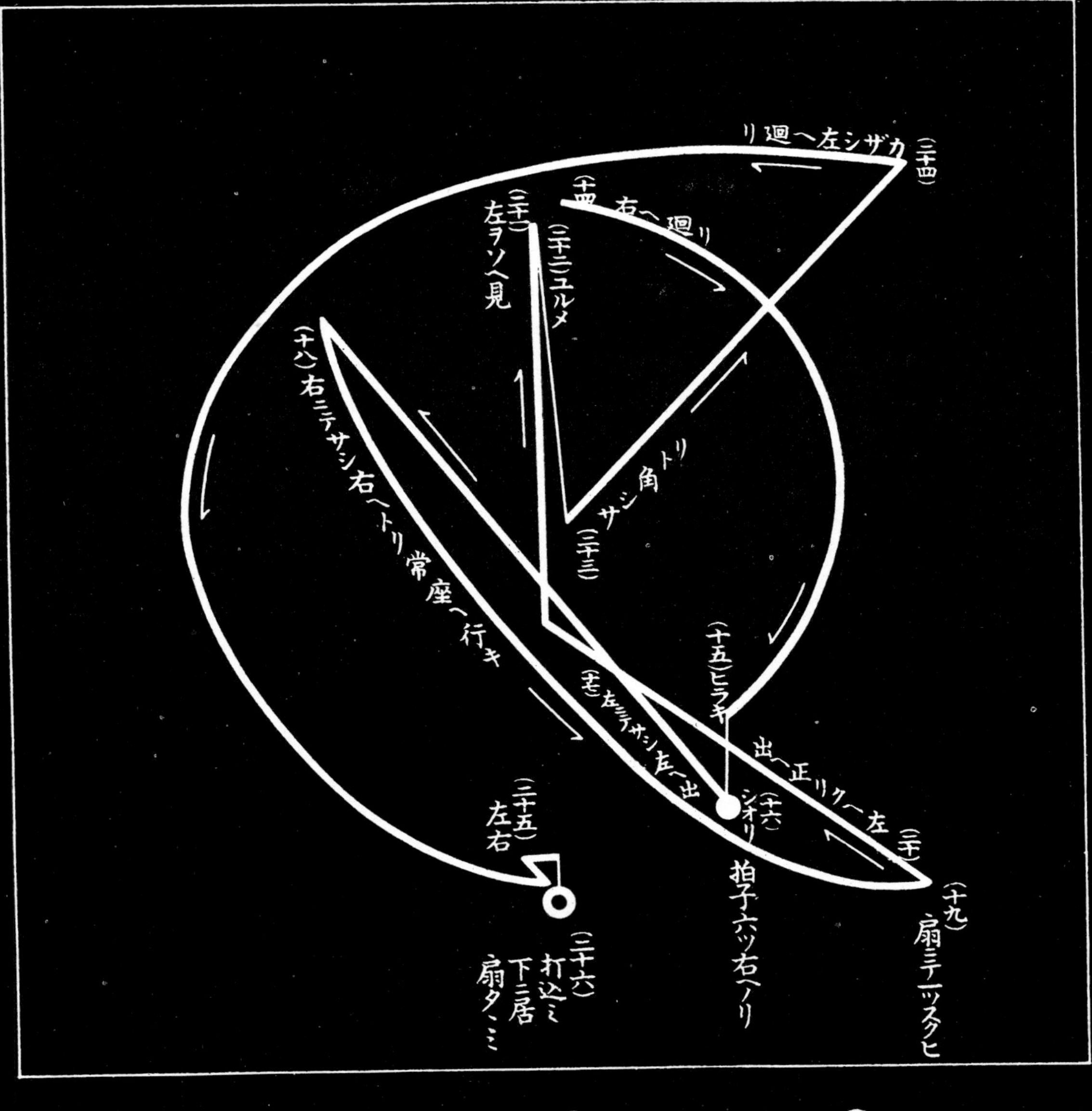

要所

(十六)拍子六ツ、三つ目より右へノリ、手を下ろす。

(十七)「花も櫻も」と左手ニテ高めをサシ、左へ出、右足に左足かけ「雪も波も」と右手ニテ低めをサシ右ヘトリ、常座へ行キ、左足に右足かける。

(十九)「すくひ集め」と扇ニテ一ツスクヒ、左ヘクリ出正中にて左手扇ヘソヘながら正先へ出、フミトメ扇を見る。

KASUGA SHRINE

Ritual dances performed in Shinto shrines contributed to the formation of the *Noh* drama.

usually, a gable roof like that of the stage at Nishi-Honganji. Extensions like verandas occur at the rear, where an alcove 9 feet deep is provided for the four musicians whose flute and drums accompany the drama, and at the right, where the stage is extended 3 feet to accommodate the chorus. The only wall in this idealized house is the backdrop for the rear alcove, which is regarded as "backstage." Painted on this wall is a large pine tree, recalling the *Noh* drama's ritual origin in forest clearings. A gallery about 20 feet long diagonally connects the backstage area to dressing rooms in an attached building. Once they have left the "room-of-the-mirror" to slowly cross this gallery the actors are on stage. Much of the narrative action, never far removed from the dance, depends on stamping and shuffling, and for centuries carpenters have refined the concealed structural details of the *Noh* stage to facilitate the amplification of sound by thirteen earthenware jars, suspended in holes dug in the ground beneath the platform. Masked and stiffly costumed, the posturing actors, as they strike the stage with their feet and sonorously recite their lines, can make the entire building rumble and boom like a giant musical instrument.

With Hideyoshi's death the Momoyama age—forty-seven years—came to an end, but the exuberance of Hideyoshi's time continued to shape the arts well into the age of the Tokugawas. This was due in part to the initial measures taken by Tokugawa Ieyasu to ensure his rule. Following the examples of Hideyoshi, Nobunaga, and the Kamakura government, Ieyasu removed himself from the intrigues of the Heian court, and around 1600, as Shogun, he made Edo his capital. Much of Edo was swampland, and great tracts were reclaimed and assigned to the nobility. An extensive strict plan on a Chinese model was not imposed, and Edo had none of Heian-kyo's orderliness. That he lacked money for land reclamation and for the enormous castle he built was for Ieyasu an advantage. He enlisted the financial aid of his vassals, who, unable to refuse, were soon so burdened with debts that they were also unable to plot uprisings against him. *Samurai* were now a hereditary caste, and to keep an eye on his feudatories Ieyasu obliged them all to spend some months of each year in the capital. When they returned to their provincial castles they were required to leave some of their women in residence at Edo. Forced to spend so much time at the capital, the nobility soon provided numerous commissions for ever larger and more luxurious mansions, and despite legislation enforcing "frugality" the common people also began to build larger and better homes. *Tatami* entirely covered the floors, all rooms were ceiled except in the poorer dwellings (and in farmhouses) and the applied arts thrived. The now idle *samurai* gave to the merchant class not only their money but also the *Shoin* style of residence, which soon lost its martial dignity. Merchants and shopkeepers came to the new capital, and the wealth fostered by peace and security, as well as by trade with Europe and China, began to make itself seen in new kinds of buildings, among them inns, restaurants, public baths, and indoor theatres. By the eighteenth century the enervating refinements of Heian-kyo and the austerities of Kamakura had indeed been escaped. The aristocratic *Noh* drama, for example, lost ground before the more colorful and boisterous *Kabuki* theatre. The people who gave excessive attention to this and other amusements were regarded as frivolous, footloose habitues of "The Floating World," which was the domain of the *Kabuki* and its immensely popular actors and actresses. Scenes from the Floating World and other agreeable quarters of Edo, as well as details of domestic life, were pictured in cheap colored prints *(ukiyo-e)* which earned the admiration of nineteenth century European connoisseurs, whereas at home they received from the Edo aristocracy only a condemnation for the vulgarity with which, it seemed, they were destroying the old standards of quality and refinement.

Ieyasu visited Kyoto from time to time, and in 1603 he built there, next to his castle, a mansion called Ninomaru, the Inner Citadel. This building consists of five units facing southwest and grouped alongside each other on a north-south axis. The first three units are directly connected to each other, but the fourth and fifth are reached by covered galleries. The arrangement combines the compact units of *Shoin* style developed by the *samurai* with the extended complexity of the Heian aristocracy's *Shinden* palaces. Grouped asymmetrically, in echelon, three of the five *Irimoya* roofs intersect in a tenuously linked but continuous composition. Each unit is approximately square, with rooms grouped in the center and surrounded by a wide wood-floored veranda. On the perimeter the veranda is enclosed by *shoji* and the wood weather-doors called *mairado;* the latter may be stored in outdoor closets at the southeast corners. There is also a narrow "wet" veranda outside, so called because it is exposed to the weather. Rooms grouped in the center of each building are of course partitioned from the enclosed veranda by *fusuma,* and servants using the verandas could walk from one end of the mansion to another without actually entering a room. But the gain in convenience also results in dimly lighted interiors, and many of the rooms are without direct ventilation. A formal entrance to the whole building is at the northeast corner, through a closed porch with a tile floor

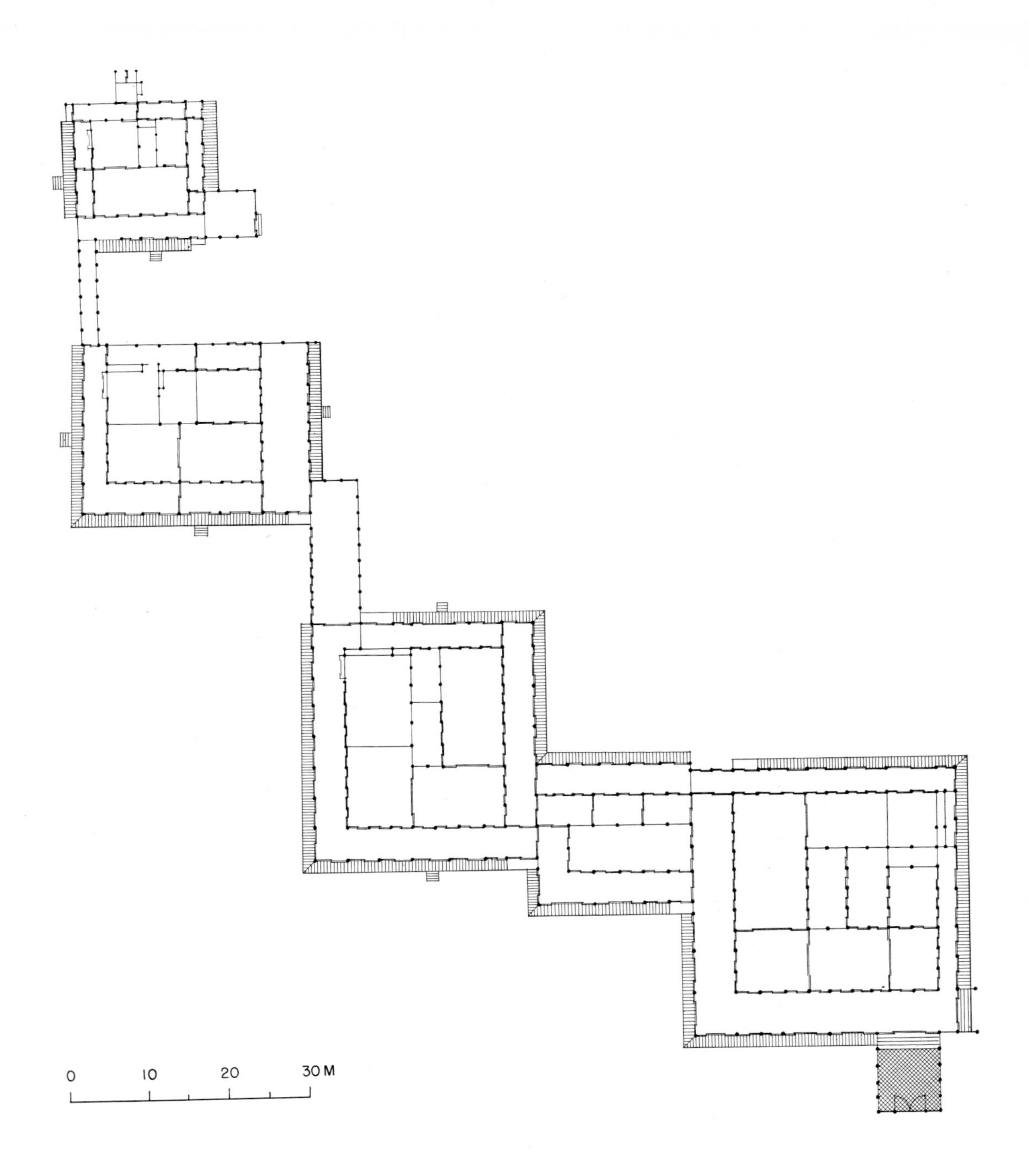

NINOMARU, NIJO CASTLE

Plan. The entrance (*genkan*) is at the lower right. The narrow outer veranda borders a closed wood-floored corridor, separated from the main rooms by sliding screens. The asymmetric arrangement of relatively small units offers an increased number of corner rooms with broad views, but the innermost rooms are without direct light or ventilation.

NINOMARU, NIJO CASTLE

A wall of white plaster screens the private garden of the first unit. The *genkan,* at the right, is roofed with *hinoki* bark shingles. Bronze decorations on the gable ends are gilded.

NINOMARU, NIJO CASTLE

The *shoji,* part wood and part paper, may be stored in outdoor closets; one of them is visible at the intersection of the two units in the background. Massive stones border the pool and are scattered in the sand gardens around it.

at ground level. Called a *genkan,* this room originated in Zen Buddhist temples, where, as the "dark place," it provided a suitable transition to the quiet rooms within a Zen establishment. Like the *shoin,* it too was borrowed by the *samurai,* but used as a hall in which to hang arms and armor. By the eighteenth century it had developed into the standard entrance, where shoes are removed, of every Japanese house.

In the first and second units of the Ninomaru are reception halls and, in the second unit, apartments for the officials who assisted the Shogun. The third unit contains the Shogun's Audience Hall, a room built on two levels like Hideyoshi's almost square Audience Hall now at Nishi-Honganji temple. But here the *shoin, tokonoma,* and *chigai-dana,* on the upper level, are at the narrow end of a room 3 *ken* wide and 9 *ken* long. Behind the Hall are private apartments and the inevitable chamber for armed guards. A further precaution against surprise manifestations of ill will is the celebrated plank flooring of the veranda itself. The planks are said to have been deliberately made to squeak, by a bevelled hard-wood spline between each board, so that slippered assassins announce themselves with a harmonious chirping from the floor.

The quality of this architecture is determined by four factors. First, the 7 foot *ken* module used makes the scale of the entire building larger than ordinary. Second, the ceilings are coved, coffered, and double coffered, giving them a plastic intricacy of scale absent from the structural framework, while for the same purpose the transoms *(ramma)* between some of the rooms are treated either as filigree bas-reliefs of plants and birds, carved on both sides, or as geometric patterns of great delicacy. Third, color applied to the ceilings, but not the structural frame, and gold applied to ornamental nail-coverings and other hardware, provide the structure with a unifying background tone illuminated by highlights. Fourth, and incorporating all of these aspects of design and decoration, paintings of mural size are used in concert with the vertical and horizontal grid of columns and *nageshi.* These structural and pseudo-structural elements, occuring in the wall plane, are isolated by painted landscapes which appear to recede or advance around them. A flatly painted branch of a tree passing behind a column may reappear as foliage brushed in dense chiaroscuro: the wall plane thus seems differently placed on either side of the column. Depth is indicated by tonality and by position with reference to the floor: a tree in the background begins higher up the wall than a tree in the foreground. But the picture plane, the actual surface, is never denied. In fact decorations are applied to it. A chrysanthemum, for example,

NINOMARU, NIJO CASTLE

The paintings of pine trees and eagles are attributed to Kano Tannyu. Gold leaf partially rubbed with white is used for the background; colors are predominantly brown, copper green, cobalt blue, and black India ink. Red and white flowers and birds on the ceiling are painted on paper or silk, pasted to the wood.

NINOMARU, NIJO CASTLE

Contrasts of dark and light are sometimes used to soften the divisions made by exposed structural framing in the wall plane. The painting of pine trees is attributed to Kano Sanraku.

This detail of Kano Sanraku's *Maple, Cypress and Peach Trees* is designed to suggest a deep space beyond the column. Repeated vertical elements make the column itself appear to occupy a point in the foreground nearest to the spectator. Because the eye sees the other verticals at depths relative to the column, the wall plane in which the column lies seems to disappear. The upper section of the wall, called *arikabe,* is here treated as part of the composition, but the narrow strip of plaster under the ceiling is left undecorated (and is not interrupted by the column) because it is intended to isolate the richly colored ceiling plane.

NINOMARU, NIJO CASTLE

Flowers, tiles, and a garden fence on these *fusuma* repeat the intricate scale of the lattice *ramma*, through which can be seen some of the ceiling decorations in the adjoining room.

Facing page, top: Above this painting of bamboo and tigers, attributed to Kano Sanraku, the *ramma* has been reduced to a narrow carved strip of flowers, leaves, and birds. Paintings on sliding screens between two rooms are often designed to destroy rather than enhance the illusion of depth. Such an emphasis of the picture plane is reinforced by making the space above the painting partially or completely open, revealing the room behind the screens.
Bottom: The base of the pine tree is cut off to suggest that it is seen from above ground level. Attention is thus diverted downward, away from the undecorated upper panels.

may be sculpturally modeled in thick impasto to introduce a "real" element, in contrast to leaves and clouds brushed with watercolor transparency.

Even when half the moveable screens are pushed behind the others, individual panels remain convincing entities. They are framed with strips of lacquer, and these divisions were also considered part of the composition, along with such minor details as hardware, so that a bole on a painted tree trunk may also coincide with the recessed hand-grip. Restricted in theme to landscapes and animals, but lavishly executed with an apparently inexhaustible invention, these paintings have perhaps been incorrectly described as decorative: at their best they are the view without which this open cage-like architecture would be incomplete.

Buddhist temples had been built customarily on flat, even sites, but the mountainous outskirts of Heian, and perhaps a certain restlessness in the life of the nation, determined the choice of irregular sites for many of the later temples. Outstanding among them is Kiyomizu, which, however, was first founded in 798, when the capital was established at Heian. Kiyomizu as it appears today was built in 1633. Its site is certainly unlikely: the oldest part of the main hall perches on Higashiyama mountain, and in front of it, flying out over the hillside, is a broad wood platform partially enclosed by two flanking galleries and a large hall. The platform is carried by an elaborate structure built of heavy columns in single lengths of timber, braced by horizontal members. The projecting ends of these braces are covered with miniature shed roofs to protect them from rain.

At the back of the main hall are rooms for priests, a sanctuary, and the long narrow altar. The major part of this hall is used by the public; such spaces date from the Heian age rather than the period of Kiyomizu's restoration, and the hall is believed to have been, originally, a palace building in Nagaoka. Except for the two side galleries projecting onto the platform the entire hall is under one great hipped roof. The gable roofs of the galleries, however, are carried around to the sides and back of the building, producing on those elevations a double roof like Todaiji's. The curves of the hipped roof are convex, but the gable roofs of the galleries are concave. This combination of gently rising and falling lines gives to the composition a slow, hovering dignity, enhanced by the natural finish of the wood. Kiyomizu is interesting for its use, however limited, of a more variously organized architectural space. A transition from the great pillared hall to the open platform is superbly achieved by the side galleries, and the building has a purposefulness to its interior design not sensed, for example, at Todaiji.

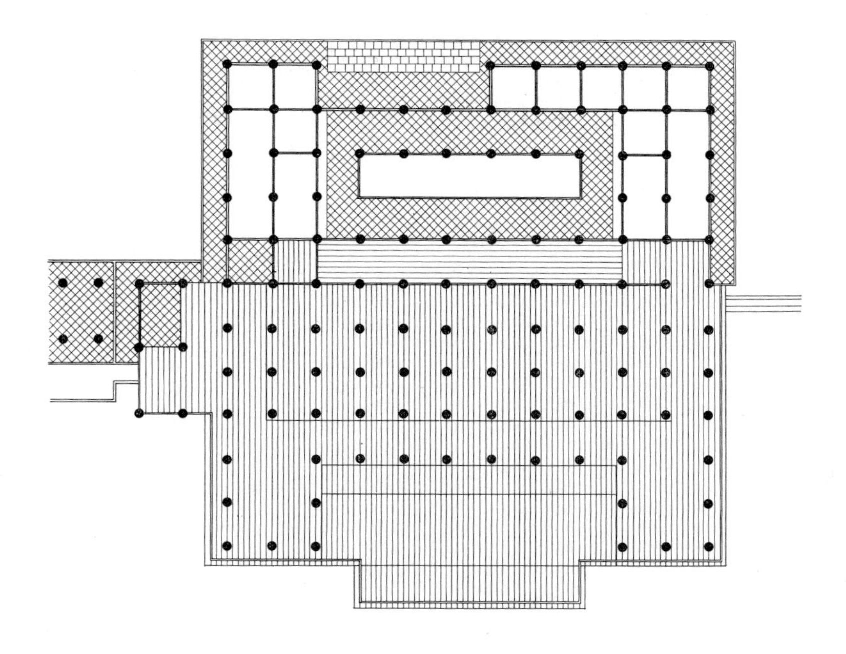

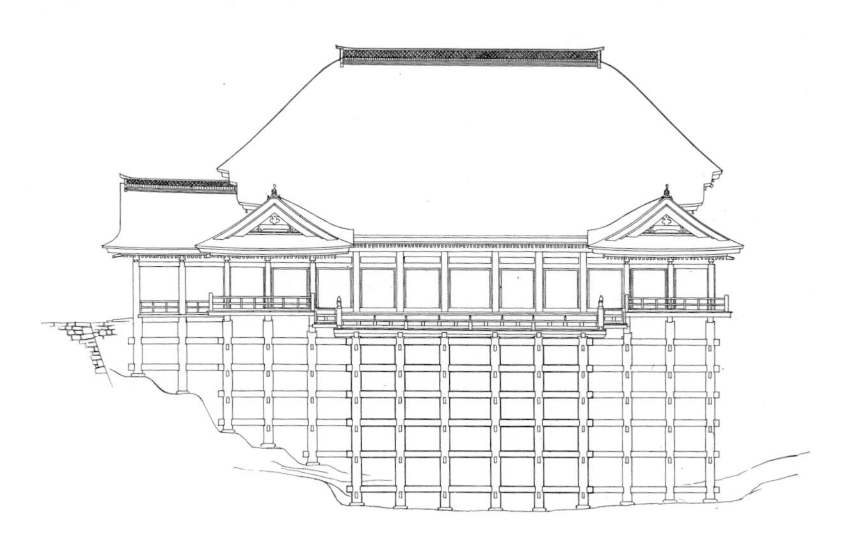

KIYOMIZU TEMPLE

Plan and elevation. Rooms for the priests and a sanctuary are shown at the top of the plan. Remaining space is used by the public.

KIYOMIZU TEMPLE

Dwelling units for the priests are connected to the main building by a covered gallery.

KIYOMIZU TEMPLE

A platform and side galleries are carried out over the hillside on a cage-like wood substructure. Convex curves of the hipped roof are a Japanese modification of concave Chinese prototypes.

NIJO CASTLE

Japanese fortifications center around a main citadel or keep, called Honmaru, which contains an observation tower and living quarters for the lord of the castle. This area is surrounded by second and third citadels, called Ninomaru and Sannomaru, and sometimes there are additional outer defenses. Stone walls supplanted earthworks during the time of Nobunaga and Hideyoshi, when European firearms were introduced to Japan. The standard height of a stone wall is twenty feet, though some are as high as one hundred and thirty feet. Stones are wedge-shaped and placed with their smaller sides turned outward. This arrangement locks them in place by their own weight, and secures them against damage by earthquake. Behind the stones a thick layer of rocks and gravel separates them from the earth core. No mortar is used, and water may escape without exerting excessive pressure.

NIJO CASTLE
Research indicates that curves were determined geometrically by formulae regarded as craft secrets. At least one expert hid work in progress behind huge bamboo curtains.

Toytomi Hideyoshi's clan contested the rule of Ieyasu, and established itself in a castle at Osaka. To meet this threat Ieyasu built castles at strategic points between Osaka and Edo. Nagoya castle, one of the most important, was given to the command of his son. After defeating the Toyotomis, Ieyasu and his successors forbade clan lords to have more than one castle each, thus reducing Japan's fortifications to little more than two hundred.

NAGOYA CASTLE

HIMEJI CASTLE

Himeji, the White Heron Castle, was in existence by the middle of the fourteenth century. It was enlarged by Hideyoshi and given its present grandeur by Ikeda Terumasu, around 1600. In addition to the main keep there are three additional tower keeps all connected by an inner corridor. The main tower has five roofs although it contains seven floors.

TURRET EAVES, HIMEJI CASTLE
The bracketing of the walls and eaves are plastered and white-washed as a protection against fire.

One country mansion and its attendant gardens and pavilions, completed around 1636, reaffirmed an attitude towards architecture neglected by such imposing works as Ieyasu's mansion at Nijo castle. Of an unassuming but deceptive simplicity, the many buildings which comprise this country estate remain today one of the major achievements of Japanese architecture, and in degrees of excellence can be compared, and contrasted, with the powerful buildings at Ise. The Katsura Villa, as it came to be known when the owner's descendants changed their family name to Katsura-no-Miya, in 1810, contains some forty-odd rooms in three connected wings. Occasionally the nearby Katsura river overflows its banks, and for safety the entire building is raised above the gently sloping ground. The eastern-most unit, called the Old Shoin, stands on slightly higher ground than the rest of the building and is raised no more than is customary for a structure of its size. The other two units, however, are held approximately 6 feet above the ground by slender stilts, recalling the ancient *Takayuka* dwelling. A white plaster wall set well back under the floor closes off the basement area to stray animals. Changes in floor level are minimized and occur chiefly at points of connection between the three units.

The units are placed asymmetrically, as they are at Nijo and as they were in an earlier version of this *Shoin-zukuri* plan, the Higashiyama Palace of the Ashikaga Shogun, Yoshimasa, where the numerous detached pavilions of *Shinden* style were simplified to make a few compact units. As developed at Katsura the *Shoin* style exploits the asymmetrical massing of units and divides interior spaces with much greater freedom and imagination. All major rooms face southeast, with rooms at the back used for circulation so that internal verandas like those at Nijo are largely omitted. Nevertheless it is not possible to traverse the entire building without stepping outside.

Katsura's *Irimoya* roofs are unusual for a building of such high social rank in that they do not imitate the flamboyant curvature of their continental predecessors. Instead, Katsura's roofs are modeled with gentle convex surfaces which, seen in profile, render their massive proportions lightly elegant and crisp. This modification in roof design is peculiarly Japanese, and at Katsura it has been further enhanced by a corresponding adjustment in the dimensions of structural members, all the columns and exposed beams being thinner than was customary for a building of such dignity.

The plan of the Katsura mansion prepared in the nineteenth century (page 148) reveals the complexity of its interior spaces. Drawn in a time-honored style, it also reveals something of the architect's system of values. In this plan the columns are clearly represented as black dots. Walls, however, are indicated only as single lines, with no attempt to differentiate between fixed or sliding walls or to indicate the number of panels on a wall made of sliding sections. It is difficult to determine from the plan alone which areas on the perimeter of the building are open and which are enclosed. An example is the unit at the upper right corner of the drawing, which represents the last part of the building to be completed. Called the New Goten, it was constructed in 1658 for the first of two visits made by the retired Emperor Gomizuno. The rooms in the New Goten are decorated with more obvious splendor than those in other parts of the building, as befitted the occasion for which they were built. The major room in the suite boasts a *shoin* on a dais, together with a sumptuous *chigai-dana*. Adjoining this room is a veranda the floor of which is partly of wood and partly of *tatami*. There is no indication on the plan that this veranda is enclosed by sliding *shoji*, or that the verandas in both the middle unit and the Old Shoin (at the left center of the plan) are entirely open. In Westernized contemporary drawings of Katsura, like the plan on page 149, sliding and fixed walls are differentiated by line weights, and the number of sliding panels for each wall is plainly shown. The earlier plan resembles in its delicacy a Paul Klee drawing, in which dots and lines patter across the page, and with its blithe indifference to everything but the location of columns the drawing expresses the architect's primary concern with compartments bounded, literally, by points of support. In the contemporary drawing the detailed organization of parts is of course clearer, but the esthetic significance of the columns is lost.

Few of the rooms in the Katsura mansion were assigned any single irrevocable function. Those few that were shaped by the specific activity they were intended to accommodate reveal a greater concern for symbolic rather than practical uses. Near the entrance to the Old Shoin there is a room where arms and armor were hung on the walls, probably as a decorative allusion to ancestral pomp, since the unfortified villa and its retiring owner evidenced little preoccupation with worldly affairs. The *shoin* room in the New Goten, with its imposing desk and shelves and its carved balustrade, served not only as a study or library but also as a formal reception room. Kitchens, in a separate wing at the rear of the building, and bath and dressing rooms were of course carefully planned utilitarian spaces. Two of the most interesting of these are storage rooms. Here the walls are divided into three tiers of shelves, all protected by sliding doors in

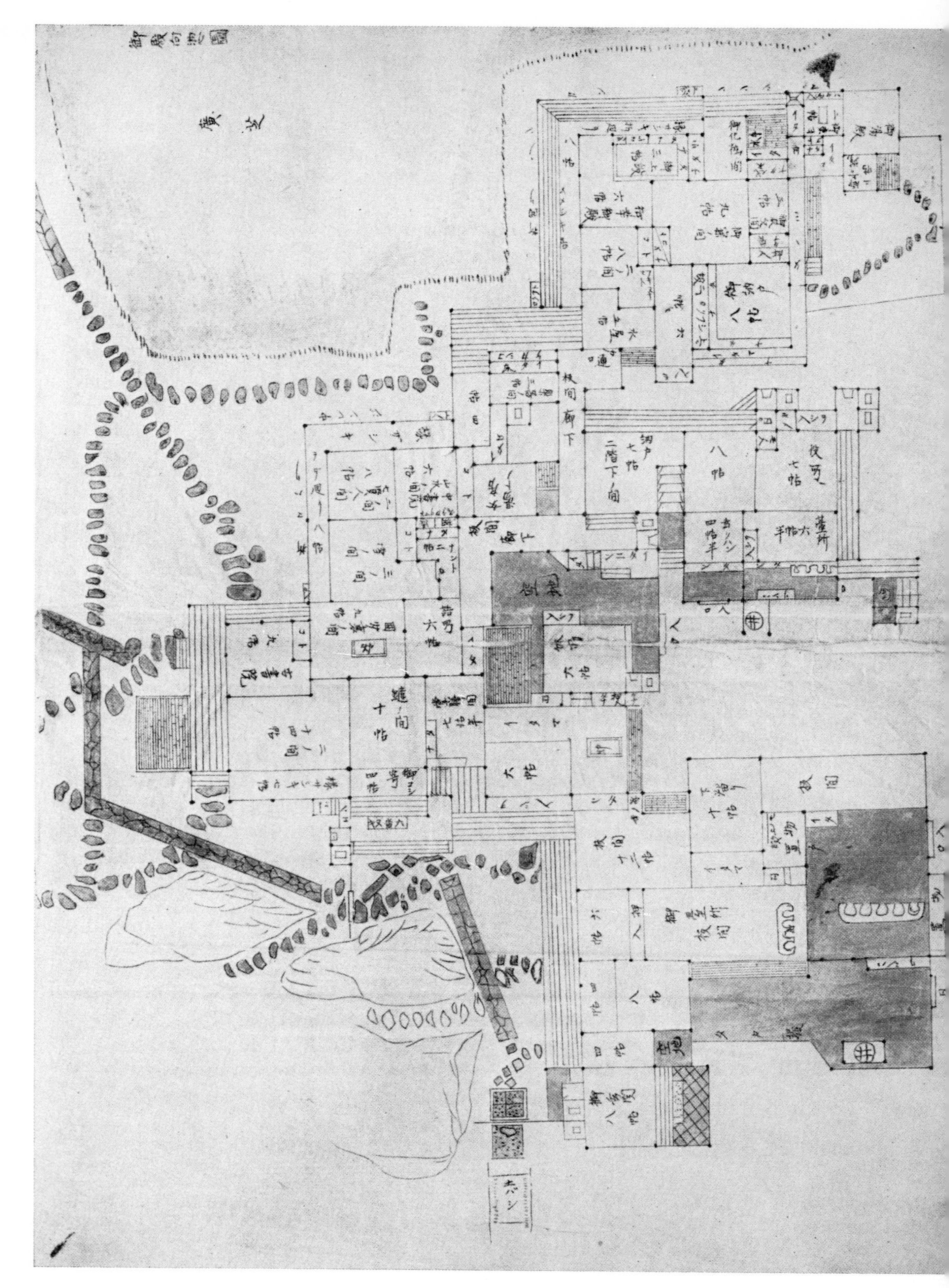

KATSURA IMPERIAL VILLA

Plan. The traditional style of this nineteenth century drawing emphasizes columns but does not distinguish different wall materials. The unit at the upper right is the New Goten, connected by a veranda to the Middle Shoin and, at the left center, the Old Shoin.

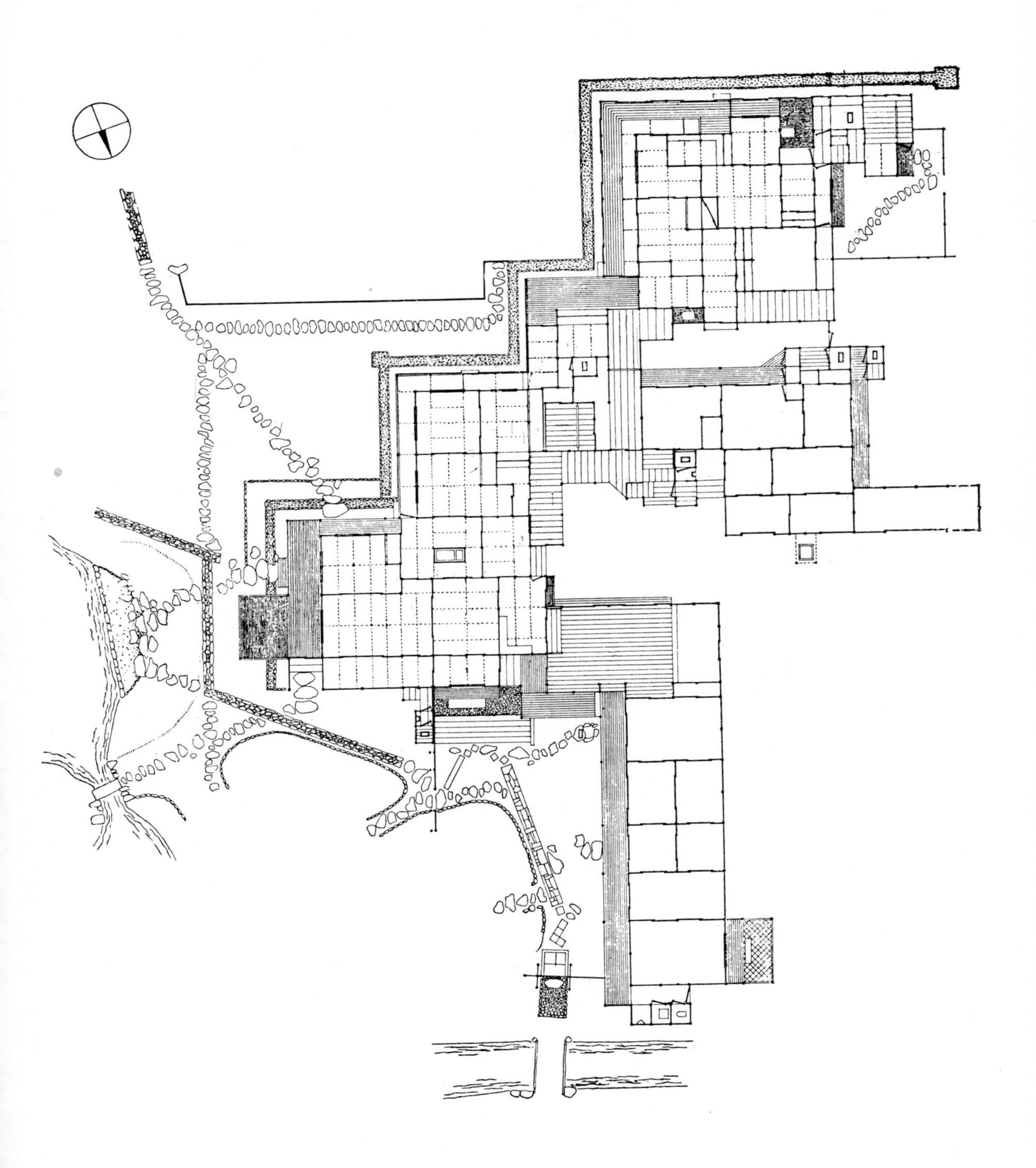

KATSURA IMPERIAL VILLA

Plan. The contemporary drawing indicates by dotted lines the number and placement of *tatami,* and differentiates sliding screens from fixed plaster walls. Kitchens and servants' quarters at the right have undergone modifications. The mansion belongs to the Imperial Household and is used briefly once a year.

KATSURA IMPERIAL VILLA

Shoes are left on the stone step outside the *genkan*.
The irregular shapes of stepping stones (left) set in moss contrast with the stone path which leads to the *genkan*. The wall at the left conceals a garden.

KATSURA IMPERIAL VILLA

The New Goten, at the far left, is connected to the Middle Shoin by a small covered veranda on which music was performed.

KATSURA IMPERIAL VILLA

The Old Shoin, at the right, has an open veranda. Stepping stones lead from the building to a landing stage at the lake.

KATSURA IMPERIAL VILLA

Sliding exterior wall panels in the Old Shoin consist of both *shoji* and wood weather doors. This arrangement admits less light but allows the unit to be completely closed.

Shoji, shown open in the photograph at the right, reveal the carved balustrade on the interior veranda of the New Goten. The closed space beneath the house is not used; a wood grille set in the plaster wall allows circulation of air. Chains hanging from the ridge allow access to the *hinoki* bark *Irimoya* roofs in case of fire. The field in front of the New Goten was used for archery and football games.

KATSURA IMPERIAL VILLA

The veranda at the left leads from the New Goten to the Middle Shoin. These units are from five to six feet above the ground.

an arrangement that anticipates by three centuries the storage wall of contemporary western usage. Clothing folded in neat squares, and personal possessions like jewel boxes, water basins, and mirrors were all kept on these shelves together with portable cabinets for other small objects. Shelves alone were adequate for clothing, since the traditional Japanese costume was not cut on the bias and was easily stored folded and flat. (But sometimes a beautiful kimono might be draped on a stand and displayed like a tapestry.) Between the middle unit and the New Goten is a veranda which was considered suitable for the outdoor performance of music, and adjacent to it is a room in which musical instruments were stored. Only a shallow ledge raised a few inches above the floor was provided for this purpose; nothing else. But the walls are covered with a pale cream-colored paper, on which is printed a shimmering pattern of silver paulownia blossoms dimly illuminated by a small vertical window.

The architectural form of Katsura is as much the reflection of one man's personality as it is the expression of attitudes widely held in Japan early in the seventeenth century. The patron who imposed his taste so effectively was Prince Toshihito. When he was ten years old the Prince, a grandson of Emperor Ogimachi, was adopted by Hideyoshi. But when a son was born to Hideyoshi in 1591 a new title was established for Toshihito and a separate mansion was built for him on the grounds of the Imperial Palace—thus elevating the Prince into a peaceful and non-political obscurity. Even as a boy, Prince Hachijo-no-Miya Toshihito showed an unusual talent for composing poetry. He was tutored by Yusai, the annotator of an anthology of verse in the Chinese and national styles, called the *Kokinshu.* On Yusai's death Hachijo-no-Miya succeeded him as guardian of the *Kokinshu* manuscripts, as well as the manuscript of Lady Murasaki's *Tale of Genji,* and became the foremost authority on their interpretation. When he decided to build a country mansion away from Heian, on the opposite bank of the Katsura river, its design naturally reflected his enthusiasm for an earlier and presumably happier age. The *Tale of Genji* is particularly rich in descriptions of country mansions, palaces, and gardens, and it appears that the Prince drew up his instructions to his gardeners and architects with these descriptions in mind. A comparison between Hachijo-no-Miya and Horace Walpole is not entirely inappropriate, but the Prince's mansion, unlike Walpole's Strawberry Hill, did not revive outmoded building forms with the casual art of a literate amateur; on the contrary, it accepted and even advanced to perfection some of the most interesting features of the sixteenth- and seventeenth-century aristocratic residence.

Attached to the veranda of the Old Shoin is a bamboo Moon Viewing platform.

KATSURA IMPERIAL VILLA
Plaster walls screen the side entrance to the veranda of the Old Shoin.

KATSURA IMPERIAL VILLA

Tokonoma in a reception room in the Old Shoin. The composition of the room depends on the juxtaposition, and the intersection at columns, of different horizontal levels. As the focal point of the room the *tokonoma* employs the strongest contrasts of heights. A narrow band of white plaster above the lattice *ramma* separates it from the ceiling and also serves to mask a change in ceiling heights.

KATSURA IMPERIAL VILLA

Tokonoma in a reception room in the Middle Shoin. In this formal design the alcove runs the width of the room, which is 12 feet, and is decorated with a painting attributed to Kano Tannyu. Shelves and storage compartments are in the alcove at the right, called *chigai-dana*. Except for the black lacquer frames and baseboards of the *tokonoma* and *chigai-dana,* all wood is the natural color, darkened by age.

KATSURA IMPERIAL VILLA
Shelves and cabinets in a reception room in the Middle Shoin.

KATSURA IMPERIAL VILLA
Tatami cover part of the floor in the enclosed veranda of the New Goten. The plaster wall, called *arikabe,* above the sliding screens, is pierced with windows which light the inner rooms when the screens are closed. Dark plaster and roughly shaped structural members are deliberately rustic. Constructed in 1658 to accommodate the visiting Emperor Gomizuno, this suite of rooms exhibits excessively decorative details.

KATSURA IMPERIAL VILLA

The desk in the main room of the New Goten is on a dais, as are the shelves and cabinets of the unusually elaborate *chigai-dana,* at the right. The low ceiling above this section of the room is coffered.

KATSURA IMPERIAL VILLA

Shelves in this wardrobe room in the New Goten can be completely closed by sliding panels. Clothing was stored folded.

A storage room in the New Goten, with open and closed shelves.

Veranda adjoining the storage room for musical instruments.

KATSURA IMPERIAL VILLA

Musical instruments were stored in the 9½ foot long *tokonoma,* at the left. A pattern of paulownia blossoms is printed in silver on the pale cream-colored wallpaper.

KARAMON GATE, TOSHOGO SHRINE

Temple architecture in the Edo period, though technically accomplished, sacrificed scale and clarity in favor of ostentatious display. Almost contemporary with Katsura, this decline of taste was fostered by the Tokugawa Shoguns in the process of deifying themselves in mausolea at Nikko. The Karamon gate of Toshogo Shrine is a characteristic example. Lacquered in brilliant colors which require constant maintenance, the building presents a surface no part of which is left undecorated.

唐門
柱には有名な
昇龍降龍の
彫刻があり屋根
には名作鵯切れの
龍・毬とがある

Superstitions once played a large part in the selection of an appropriate site, for whole cities as well as for private houses. Collected in books of charts and instructions called *Kaso,* most of these injunctions contain eminently practical advice. The classical *Kaso* diagram is a circle around which are disposed the months and seasons of the year like the numbers on a clock or the cardinal points of a compass. At the north is December (winter); at the east is March (spring); June is at the south (summer); and at the west is September (autumn). All twelve months are represented on the circle by lines radiating from its center, and on each of these axes are entered, by means of six short lines, all the information one requires. For instance, December, the month of the Rat, is marked by one broken line nearest the perimeter of the circle, the other five lines being unbroken. This means, among other things, that very little sunlight can be expected to penetrate the circle during December, though there will be more than in November, which has unbroken lines only and so admits no sun at all. May, on the other hand, is like an open door: all the lines are broken and sunlight streams in. January, the month of the Ox, and February, the month of the Tiger, are in a direction best closed off against evil spirits. The roots first take hold in December and by January they have absorbed enough water to produce dampness: therefore one should be careful about the northeast (as well as the southwest). The most auspicious direction for a house to face is southeast. April and May fall in that quarter of the circle and eleven of their twelve lines are broken, thus admitting the maximum amount of sunlight. The Katsura mansion faces southeast, as do thousands of farmhouses in comparable latitudes all over the world, but Ieyasu's Kyoto mansion faces southwest. Some of the *Kaso* injunctions suggest a mixture of superstitious and esthetic, rather than practical, motives: according to the rules of *Kaso* houses are best placed with a mountain to the rear and a valley in front, to cut off the more serious demonic assaults. Aside from the instincts to self preservation that may underlie an esthetic response to this arrangement, we may recognize it as a composition which controls visually a building's approach and background.

The Japanese have always regarded buildings as aspects of the natural scene. Unlike the Greeks or the Chinese they have never attempted seriously the creation of an architecture complete and valid unto itself, no matter where in the landscape it is set down. Mountains in Japan were never thought to be uncouth, as the English once liked to regard the attractions of Switzerland, but on the other hand nothing could be more alien to the Japanese temperament than the

POND GARDEN, SAIHOJI TEMPLE
Stones are placed in and around the Golden Pond of Saihoji Temple's small pond garden. The ground is entirely covered with moss.

allées of Versailles, or the symmetrical plateaus and busy fountains of the great Italian gardens. The background of architecture in Japan is not a garden merely but mountains and fields and, indirectly, the sea. Water and islands, the sense of seascape, inform the Japanese gardener's art with a theme partially religious in origin (Emperor Nintoku's tomb was an island surrounded by three moats). The major classifications under which Japanese gardens may be described, with the exception perhaps of gardens for tea pavilions, are the pond garden and the *Kare-sansui* (mountain and water) garden. Pond gardens begin their long and circuitous development with islands in the center of a lake, often immense, and in the sixth century a garden was called simply *magario,* a curved beach. The islands were held to be sacred abodes of the deceased. Sometimes there were four or more islands strung out in a line (like Japan itself), the formation being designated the "archipelago style." Royal dwellings or shrines were placed on the islands, rather than on the shore, presumably for security. Amplification of the shapes and sizes of these islands produced the "dragonfly style," with one or two islands shaped like dragonflies placed so that their arms formed paths to the shore. When houses were built on the shore rather than on the islands the latter became entirely ornamental.

During the Heian period a Buddhist legend concerning a mythical island in the farthest reaches of the sea, where one could find eternal youth, enjoyed a great vogue through ornamental *Horai* islands intended to represent this paradise. Cranes and turtles, symbols of long life, suggested more interesting shapes and eventually replaced the earlier Buddhist symbol. Throughout the Heian age the largest of these "boating gardens" provided the decor for royal progressions gliding over the water to impeccable islands. The Katsura palace itself was the scene of such excursions: Hachijo-no-Miya, and afterwards his heir, Prince Toshitada, on summer evenings stepped from the terrace before the Old Shoin into a painted boat: passing first under a red bridge now vanished, he sailed away to the tea pavilion called Shoiken, on a promontory where fireflies were especially thick in that season, and perhaps, after a musician had sung the appropriate song, he admired the lantern lights at the more elegant Shokintei, and late at night returned past Orindo, the Buddhist temple in which was kept a portrait of Hachijo-no-Miya's literary mentor, Yusai. Even if they were sustained by too elaborate mechanics, and lacked a certain spontaneity, these were Cytherean journeys Watteau would have admired.

These dreamlike landscapes were replaced by a new

GARDENS OF KATSURA IMPERIAL VILLA

At the left is a small island connected to the mainland by a stone bridge. The lantern at the right stands on the edge of a promontory surfaced with smooth round stones, representing a pebble beach. The Old Shoin may be seen in the background.

kind of garden in which their chief charm was embodied. If the new aristocracy, the warrior class, austere and economical, reduced the size of the garden to something more reasonably maintained, they nevertheless preserved the idea of moving through it, albeit on foot, in a carefully planned tour of its attractions. Greater attention to detail in a confined space eventually produced the "scenery garden," in which famous scenes were reproduced in specific, realistic detail. As in the *Noh* drama, realism meant a transposition of the world of nature beyond the garden (which belongs to art) into manageable, stylized fragments. Thus in a garden representing a view of the ocean, selected stones were arranged along the edge of the pond to represent crashing breakers. Stones were used to represent even mist, in the shapes often found in Chinese monochrome paintings. Sometimes a famous view might be summarized by a single object, and in a "condensed scenery garden" one pine tree might symbolize a whole forest. Or the treatment might be reversed to include not only the contents of the garden but also "borrowed scenery," like a neighbor's bamboo grove, or distant mountains.

By the fifteenth century the space immediately in front of a house, customarily reserved for ceremonial purposes, was often made into a small garden designed to be seen only from the main rooms of the building. Undoubtedly the need to economize spurred the development of walled "mountain and water" gardens in which there were neither water nor mountains, and sometimes indeed no living thing. But war, pestilence, and poverty only gave practical point to a re-creation of nature that was already symbolic. Many of the ideas developed during this time had first been displayed in the pond garden, and to these were added some new themes drawn from temples and shrines. Like other ceremonial sites, temple compounds were strewn with a coarse white sand. At one end of the area a reserve supply of this sand was pressed into a truncated cone. Eventually, Japanese gardeners believe, this cone of surplus sand was admired for its decorative effect, and sand itself was seen as a gardener's medium. In "dry" gardens, mostly rectangular, the sand might be spread irregularly and the margins filled with moss, clipped trees, or shrubs. A wall of plaster or board usually enclosed three sides of the plot: within this frame the gardener "painted" a picture, using stones for brushstrokes. The analogy is authentic: one of the most striking of the *Kare-sansui* styles is the "pictorial," in which the brushwork of Chinese black ink paintings was deliberately imitated. To compensate for the distortion brought about by having the "picture plane" stretch away from the observer,

POND GARDEN, SHUGAKUIN IMPERIAL VILLA

The forty-acre gardens of Shugakuin, completed in 1653, are part of a vast Imperial estate outside Kyoto, which is hidden from view by the Western Mountains in the background at the left. What appear to be clipped shrubs covering the field in the foreground are actually trees twelve feet high. Gardeners climb ladders placed between the branches to keep the tops evenly clipped. The low hedge bordering a path on the far side of the lake is in reality approximately five feet high and seven feet wide. Both in its scale and in the gentle sweep of its contours the garden suggests an English park.

GARDEN OF DAISEN-IN, DAITOKUJI TEMPLE

Detail. This garden has undergone numerous changes since it was first designed in 1513. Vertical stones in the background represent a mountain waterfall, and stones are also used to represent cliffs and a boat.

along the ground, predominantly vertical shapes were grouped at the rear and the ground itself was often pitched downward imperceptibly toward the veranda, from which the garden is seen. At Daitokuji Temple, in the garden of Daisen-in, one of the most convincing of these compositions despite the alterations it has suffered, there is a white plaster wall, now half hidden, that once carried the tone of the sand-strewn ground up behind all the clipped shrubs, thus flattening onto an imaginary picture plane objects in reality some distance from each other. At Daisen-in too can be seen several other characteristics of the dry garden. For example, two boulders are balanced on end to suggest, by the narrow space between them, a mountain waterfall. Before this group, and nearer to the spectator, is a stone bridge crossing what is meant to be a narrow ravine through which water (moss) rushes wildly. In the foreground a stone boat bobs about, and along the sides of the stream are steep stone cliffs against which lumps of moss symbolically foam. Because the waterfall is supposed to be a great distance away the trees behind it are smoothly clipped: the stone bridge, which indicates the middle distance, is much larger in scale, and trees in the foreground, also larger in scale, are left untrimmed so that they may have the detail one expects to see near at hand.

The most beautiful of all sand gardens is that belonging to Ryōanji Temple, near Kyoto. Ryōanji was a Zen Temple established on a site previously held by another sect, and its famous sand garden was designed in 1499, when a house was built for the new superior. After this building was destroyed by fire in 1797 a similar one was put up on the same site; the garden is not believed to have been altered. On three sides a plaster wall, part of it rubbed with oil, encloses the rectangular plot; the fourth side of this imaginary picture frame is provided by the veranda, and behind that the rooms, of the superior's house. Only from these rooms and the veranda can the garden be seen. It can not be entered. The garden consists simply of fifteen stones arranged in twos, threes, and fives, totaling five groups in all. Some moss at the base of each group softens the contrast with the white sand. There are no trees, sand covers the whole area, and a shallow trench made of cut stones provides a neat border. What is it that accounts for the tension generated by this space? In part it is the site itself. Ryōanji is some distance from Kyoto, in a forest on a hillside. From the veranda one looks over the garden wall at tree tops thin against the sky. There is no sound, not even from the village below, and the centuries conspire to make the visitor's response appropriately subjective.

But there is also a structure that reveals itself slowly, and the beauty of this garden is not entirely an accident of circumstances.

Traditionally the elements of *Kare-sansui* gardens were composed in triangles rather than on formal axes. Three stones or trees in a triangle refer vaguely to Buddha and his two consorts. Usually six objects, or groups of objects, would be arranged as the points of two separate but adjacent triangles, and the gardener's artfulness was spent in adjusting their relationships—no two of which are likely to be the same. At Ryōanji, however, it is believed that a slightly different device was employed. There seem to be two basic triangles overlapping each other, and one group of stones constitutes simultaneously the apex of two or more superimposed triangles. Lines drawn between all the points of any two triangles, adjacent or superimposed, will of course produce several more triangles. But the key to Ryōanji's composition may be determined, according to taste, by settling on a particular group of stones as the apex of one triangle (the Buddha in the triumvirate), thus establishing the order of the remaining points. Regardless of how the garden's formal structure is interpreted, its field of empty space remains a tangible sign of Zen Buddhist speculation; austere, deliberate, and perhaps bitter.

The spiritual content of stone compositions was not originally so exalted. In the seventh century the Imperial Court received as a gift from the Emperor of China a collection of curiously shaped stones. So great was the enthusiasm for such things that there was invented a kind of parlor game—perhaps it should be likened to solitaire—in which small stones were arranged in a lacquer tray filled with sand. Called *bonseki,* these tray landscapes were an amusing rule-ridden preparation for later essays in design more ambitious and expensive. Stones of bizarre shapes, suggesting all sorts of things, were dug up and dragged at great expense from remote provinces to ornament what had once been small and economical gardens. Ryōanji's stones do not belong to this category, except insofar as they were selected for their sculptural qualities, but they are distinguished by a consistency of texture and scale one might expect to find in an ink drawing executed with an almost dry brush.

GARDEN OF RYŌANJI TEMPLE
Five groups of stones set in moss are arranged on a field of white sand. Part of the wall is rubbed with oil. The garden may be seen only from the veranda.

Just as *tatami* give the floors of Japanese houses an unexpected interest, it is the texture and modeling of the ground that gives to most Japanese gardens their peculiarly insistent tactile qualities. Traditional footwear—the wood clogs called *geta*—impose a short abrupt step. This is exploited by the gardener through surface materials which determine the pace at which a garden may be inspected. Conscious always of the path he must follow, and alert to keep his balance as he makes his way through carefully plotted sequences of moss, widely spaced stepping stones, dried pine needles, rocks, narrow bridges, smooth pavement, and coarse gravel, the spectator's attention is necessarily directed to the ground. Perhaps the most encyclopedic array of textural sequences is to be found in the gardens of Katsura. It is true that here the insistence on titillating surprises is sometimes tiresome, and that the gardens lack the single compelling feature that would have given them dramatic coherence (although the missing red bridge may once have provided this). But in variety and invention Katsura's gardens are unsurpassed. From no two angles does any part appear quite the same; like the bits of paper and glass inside a kaleidoscope, Katsura's trees, stones, ponds, and buildings tumble into fresh patterns merely by the act of moving through them.

Another pastime elevated by the Japanese to the realm of creative expression, but one which remains largely incomprehensible to the West as an art form, is the arrangement of flowers. The rules for flower compositions, with their first and second subjects and major and minor themes, are no less elaborate than were those for the game of *bonseki*. Both pursuits reflect certain characteristic preoccupations of the Japanese landscape artist. One of the most striking of these is the great store set on the unique and preferably venerable object. Objects not sufficiently unique are often made so, either by distorting the object itself or by subtly altering the context in which one expects to see it. Ordinary trees in a temple courtyard or a private garden, for example, sometimes seem strangely independent of the ground out of which they have sprung, because the ground level has been built up and perhaps covered with a layer of white sand or gravel, thus concealing the roots and making the greenish-black trunks seem like decorative accessories pinned to a carpet. In many gardens twisted stones vie for attention with twisted trees so old that their limbs must be supported by bamboo crutches. Set apart by a low granite fence in the courtyard of Nishi-Honganji Temple is one such venerable pine tree, its branches, extending perfectly horizontal for twenty feet, held aloft on all sides by a forest of bamboo

GARDENS OF KATSURA IMPERIAL VILLA
At the end of a road paved with small stones is a promontory on which stands a pine tree, drawing attention to an excellent view of the lake.

OVERLEAF
Right: Stepping stones set in moss.
Left: Stepping stones set in rocks.

GARDENS OF KATSURA IMPERIAL VILLA

To make visitors pause at the entrance steps the stone path leading to the *genkan* abruptly changes direction, scale, and texture. The area without moss is designed to connect visually both sections of the path.

Stone bridge in the garden of the Katsura Imperial Villa.

GARDENS OF KATSURA IMPERIAL VILLA
Diamond-shaped stepping stones relate a building to a stone path which parallels the veranda.

A stone path fifty-four feet long and three feet wide is terminated by a water basin at one end and a lantern at the other. "Parting stones" along the way lead to other paths or buildings.

GARDENS OF KATSURA IMPERIAL VILLA
This water basin adjoins a Buddhist temple on an island in Katsura's gardens. Moss, pebbles, and grass are combined with cut stone.

The cut stone basins at the lower left are part of the cooking equipment in Katsura's Shokintei tea pavilion. Irregular stepping stones are used for maximum contrast but are related to the lawn by a gradual change in texture from small pebbles to moss. The stone curb indicates a boundary. The composition is one of many variations on the dot and line theme used throughout Katsura's gardens.

Water basin in the gardens of the Katsura Imperial Villa.

GARDENS OF KATSURA IMPERIAL VILLA

Stone water basin under the eaves of the Shoiken tea pavilion. The weight and sculptural mass of the large stones is emphasized by the smaller curved stones, which seem to be rising out of a pit. A path at the foot of the hill is bordered with small stones to make a dotted line.

GARDEN OF SAMBOIN TEMPLE

Circles of moss are set in a field of white sand. The garden was redesigned in its present form in 1698, for a feast given by Hideyoshi. Although the moss circles are perhaps its most interesting detail, the garden also contains stones so highly regarded that they were wrapped in brocade while being carried to the site.

MOSS BRIDGE, SAMBOIN TEMPLE

Boulders are used for abutments, and two beams carry a deck made of logs packed with clay. Moss planted on this surface and on the banks of the pond makes the bridge appear to be a ribbon of earth stretched across the water.

poles that all but conceals the tree itself. The limbs of trees are often tied to the ground, to buildings, to adjacent trees, and clipped, bent, or otherwise coaxed toward distinction. Three blossoms on the stalk must be removed to make more perfect the already perfect fourth, and sometimes the stalk itself must be broken to render its line more poignantly expressive. Landscapes in pots, miniature trees with jade bridges, are other expressions of this enthusiasm.

But the products of this aspect of Japanese sensibility are not always miniature or painfully exquisite. An example is the garden of Jishoji temple. If Ryōanji is the most beautiful of *Kare-sansui* gardens, the garden of Jishoji temple and Ginkakuji, the Silver Pavilion, is certainly the most astonishing. It was to the Silver Pavilion on a hill near Kyoto that the Ashikaga Shogun, Yoshimasa, withdrew to contemplate his collection of ceramics and paintings, compose poetry, and study the *Noh* drama. The Silver Pavilion, in modest imitation of the Golden Pavilion built by Yoshimasa's grandfather, was to have been covered entirely with silver leaf, including its bark roof, but it was never quite finished. At the beginning of the Edo period the estate became the property of Jishoji temple, and a sand garden was added near the pond originally made for the Silver Pavilion. The Edo period addition consists of a cone of sand some 14 feet in diameter at the base and approximately 6 feet high, and a broad triangular plateau of sand about 30 inches above the ground. The cone symbolizes a mountain, while the plateau, its surface raked in a pattern of straight lines, symbolizes the ocean. This conjunction of shapes a little too large for the area is disturbing. Jishoji's garden, however, is a no less disciplined expression of the sculptor-gardener's art than is Ryōanji's, and the discordant scale is perhaps its particular refinement. But where Ryōanji is designed to compel silence and the contemplation of what is essentially incommunicable, Jishoji is designed to provoke comment. The spirit of Zen Buddhism had changed over the years.

The *tokonoma,* the *shoin,* and the *genkan* were all architectural features of Zen buildings, borrowed in a spirit of respect and admiration by the *samurai* for their own use, and eventually adapted throughout Japan. But Zen influence was far more profound than these superficial details may suggest, and in order to understand the architecture of the tea house, perhaps the strongest expression of Zen attitudes, it is necessary to know something of Zen itself. By the sixth century Buddhism in India had produced two major schools, the Mahayana and the Hinayana. Both schools had in common the belief that man suffers because he desires to retain what is essentially impermanent: his life, his possessions,

GARDEN OF JISHOJI TEMPLE

An early Edo period addition to an Ashikaga garden, the plateau called Ginshanada and a cone of sand represent, respectively, a moonlit sea and a mountain. The railing in the foreground is a contemporary addition. Ginkakuji, Yoshimasa's Silver Pavilion, may be seen in the background.

GINKAKUJI, JISHOJI TEMPLE
The Silver Pavilion, overlooking a pond garden.

GARDEN OF JISHOJI TEMPLE
Cone of sand in the garden of Jishoji Temple.

Women picking tea leaves.

and beautiful things. The self was regarded by the Hinayanists as truly non-existent—an illusion—while the Mahayanists maintained that when man renounced his false self he would discover the true one, and that the true self included within it the whole universe. This state of being one with the universe was called *Nirvana,* while the world of changing forms in which we live was called the Many: the Wheel of Birth and Death. For the Hinayanist the highest spiritual attainment was escape from the self to the One: *Nirvana.* But to the Mahayanist the eternal peace of *Nirvana* is impossible to enjoy while others suffer. Thus the Mahayanist must renounce what may have taken innumerable successive lives to attain, so that he can return to the world of forms and help others to find enlightenment and release.

The Zen sect saw the distinction between the One and the Many as a necessary defect of language, or more precisely of the intellect, and maintained that *Nirvana* exists here, now, in everything, but that it can be apprehended only by a direct intuitive grasp, and that intellectual approaches can lead only to partial, and hence false, understanding. Little is known of Zen in India. The first great Zen teacher, Bodhidharma, appeared in China in A.D. 527, at which time he explained to the Emperor Wu that there was no special merit in building temples, since everything in the world was already holy. Distressed by this news the Emperor querulously desired to know by what right, therefore, did Bodhidharma come to lecture him on holiness, and Bodhidharma eagerly conceded that he had no idea what he was doing there. According to a famous legend Shang Kwang, Bodhidharma's disciple, waited in the snow outside the cave in which the master sat meditating. He waited for several years without gaining the master's attention. Then, to demonstrate his perseverance by a gesture which could not fail to be noticed, he cut off his frostbitten arm and presented it to Bodhidharma, who murmured, "I see you are serious." Zen in China absorbed much of the teaching of Lao Tzu, and when it was established in Japan by Essai, in 1191, it embodied many of the great Chinese philosopher's recommendations about the Tao, the process of living (the Way). Because of their weightless spiritual enlightenment Zen teachers found it impossible to take too seriously the gross but transient things of this world, and so they necessarily appeared quixotic. Often they helped their students attain enlightenment, which had to come instantaneously, by sudden slaps and kicks, and enlightenment was tested by the response to riddles impossible to answer logically. Chinese and Japanese artists unfailingly pictured Bodhidharma as a gruff black-bearded man with bushy eyebrows, staring at

TEA BOWL AND TEA WHISK

Shown approximately two thirds its actual size, this contemporary sand colored tea bowl of traditional design is partially covered with a translucent whitish glaze. Irregularities in shape and texture are part of its distinction. The tea whisk, made from a single piece of bamboo, is used to mix powdered tea.

the world with comic ferocity. No doubt training in Zen did sharpen the sense of humor.

Tea, like Zen, also came from China. It had been used there since the eighth century, and was carried to Japan by merchants and returning scholars. People of the T'ang dynasty packed the tea leaves into a moist cake which they later boiled; Sung enthusiasts ground the leaves into a green powder which, with the aid of a bamboo tea whisk, was whipped into a brew the consistency of split-pea soup; and Ming esthetes steeped the leaves in boiled water to produce what we know today as tea. Zen monks drank tea together before an image of Bodhidharma, and tea was taken often during the long periods spent in meditation. Eventually the Zen monasteries set aside special rooms in which the monks took their tea with less solemnity, and by the fifteenth century, under the enthusiastic patronage of the Ashikaga Shogun, Yoshimasa, the tea ceremony was established on a secular basis. Tea was considered to be of medical as well as mystical advantage: it cleansed the body, it purified the mind, and in general it encouraged right thinking.

At first the space set aside in private homes for the tea ceremony was not more than four and one half mats—about 9 feet square—this being the amount of space in which a legendary Buddhist figure received a saint and his 86,000 disciples, in a demonstration of the non-existence of space to the truly enlightened. Not more than five persons, however, were expected to participate, and a portable screen shielded the tea area from the rest of the room. The first independent tea house was designed late in the sixteenth century by Sen-no-Rikyu, under the patronage of Hideyoshi. In addition to the tea room itself Rikyu provided a separate pantry, where some of the materials were prepared, a shelter in which guests assembled until summoned to enter the tea house, and, connecting the two, a garden path so landscaped as to remove from the minds of those who walked it all thoughts of the world outside.

The tea ceremony, called *cha-no-yu,* encourages its participants to delight in simple, homely activities, and in beautiful surroundings, including the objects used in the tea service, and to appraise works of art intelligently. To facilitate this mood of respectful but enthusiastic estheticism every phase of the ceremony was strictly prescribed, the guests having agreed on the order in which they would enter the pavilion while they were still waiting in the garden; and the mixing, serving, and drinking of tea, as well as the studied approval of the kettle and bowls and the decorations in the alcove, were all conducted according to plan. These prescriptions were, it will be readily imagined, multitudi-

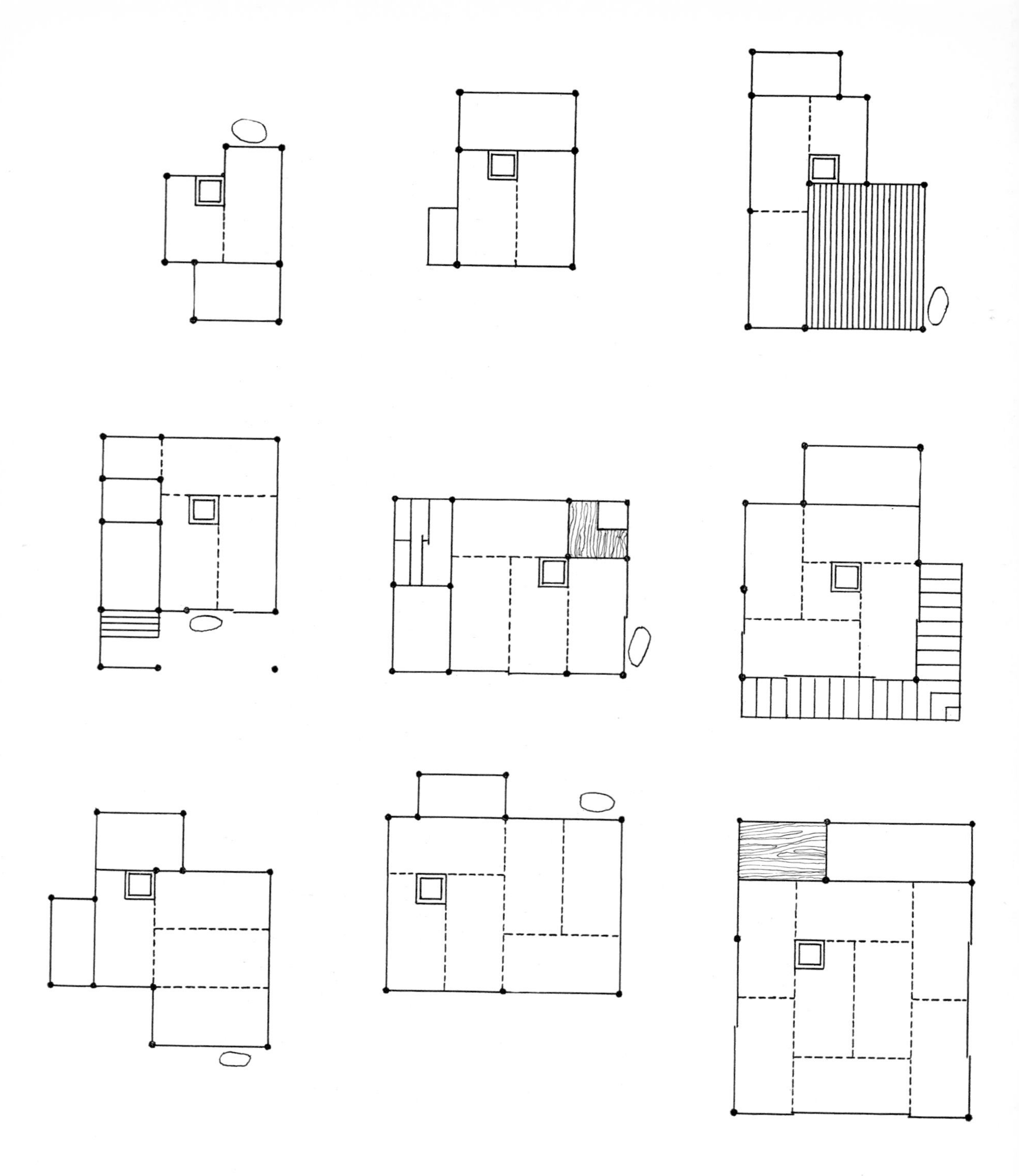

TEA ROOM PLANS

The small square in each plan represents the hearth. Plans range in size from a three mat room (top left) in which two of the mats are three-quarter length, to a nine mat room (bottom right) in which one mat adjoining a *tokonoma* is 1¼ *ken* long.

HOUSE FOR TEA CEREMONY
Stepping stones lead to a small "crawling-in entrance," intended to make guests disassociate themselves from the outside world through the inconvenience they must momentarily endure, regardless of rank. The main roof is of thatch.

JO-AN TEA ROOM
A wood partition partially screens the hearth; here and in the *tokonoma* at the left, columns are made of unfinished wood. Tracks for sliding panels divide the wall into three tiers.

nous. Tea masters famed for the subtlety with which they created an appropriate atmosphere soon became arbiters of taste, influencing through their patrons the development of painting and literature. The black ink paintings of the Ashikaga period, for example, owe some of their allusive white emptiness to the taste of the tea masters, as does the metaphysically significant emptiness of Ryōanji's sand garden. The tea house itself was intended as a demonstration of Zen (and Taoist) attitudes. Lao Tzu had remarked that the true reality of a room was not its walls but the emptiness they contained. The only reality, Lao Tzu said, is nothingness: a room is inconceivable unless it be—nothing. Therefore the purest style of tea house architecture, called *Sukiya-zukuri* (*sukiya* may be translated variously as the abode of fancy or the abode of nothingness) claimed to be concerned not with the material of the building itself but with the emptiness within. To proclaim this more persuasively the buildings were made of rude materials. Walls were not finished with white plaster, as they would be in a house, but were left the natural color of the earth. Ceilings were of bamboo and roofs were of thatch, and often at least one of the columns would be an imperfectly finished, if not entirely rough, tree trunk from which the bark had not been removed. Kokuzo Okakura, in his famous *Book of Tea,* remarks that teaism is "essentially worship of the Imperfect." It was important to produce a space that would reflect the transiency of things in this world, the world of forms, and to this end asymmetrical compositions were preferred: only what is incomplete is still within the process of life (the Way) and is therefore imperfect (asymmetrical).

The rough, country materials of the tea house, which often adjoined an ineffably luxurious mansion, were also intended to affirm man's oneness with nature. Needless to say mere crudity was not enough, and a well-constructed tea pavilion was a very expensive building indeed. Months might be spent in selecting the right twisted tree trunk and an earth of suitable color (red-ochre from Kyoto is still considered superior) and the finished buildings were rather like fine cabinets in their delicacy and precision.

While the main developments of architecture in Japan were concerned with the articulation of structure, *sukiya* architecture used structure primarily as a point of departure for decorative effects. Like Japanese houses, tea pavilions were built of light wood frames, but the frames were filled mostly with walls of earth applied to a lath of bamboo. Whole walls of translucent *shoji* were infrequently used because the atmosphere of refinement calls for a subdued light, and because the small space makes solid walls desir-

TAI-AN TEA ROOM, MYOKI-AN TEMPLE

Designed in 1582 by the famous tea master Sen-no-Rikyu, Tai-an has ochre colored plaster walls mixed with pieces of straw for textural interest. Exposed wood members are left partially unfinished. At the corner of the room on the left and at the back of the *tokonoma* structural members have been entirely concealed.

The bamboo lath has been left exposed to make a decorative lattice for the window. The bamboo pole which bisects it is actually part of the column structure reinforcing the wall.

SHOKINTEI, KATSURA IMPERIAL VILLA
The arched doorway at the left leads to a pantry. Placement of windows is partially determined by lighting requirements during the tea ceremony. White paper pasted to the wall at floor level protects it from fingermarks. Shelves attached to the wall are held at the corner by a bamboo pole suspended from the ceiling. As in Tai-an, columns are concealed wherever they might detract from the importance of a few major vertical elements, such as the rough, curved center-post used here.

able if only as backgrounds for the occupants of the room. The skeleton structure makes it possible to cut windows in any part of these earth walls, and the practical incentive to do this came from the need for a strong light at specific points in the room; near the hearth, for example, where the host may be mixing the tea. Thus the windows were used almost as stage lights carefully arranged at all levels to pick out certain phases of the performance. To illustrate rustic oneness with nature, and an indifference to the appearance of things, a window might be placed so that it was casually interrupted by a column. An example is found in the pavilion called Tai-an, at Myoki-an temple. The bamboo lath has here been left intact to make a lattice for the window opening; but the exposed bamboo "column" is of dubious structural value. Windows on the same wall might be arranged in tiers, the tracks being carried straight across the wall and the different panels either wallpapered, below, or left plain. At Tai-an the alcove set aside for a work of art is unusual for its rounded corners, which deliberately conceal the structure in an effect hard to consider casual, or rustic, despite the fact that pieces of straw have been mixed with the earth to give the walls a pastoral texture.

Simplicity so carefully prepared tends to become tiresome, and ends by being most complicated. Often these decorative effects are beautiful, but equally often they are related more to painting or graphic design than to architecture. Yet *sukiya* architecture provided a means of developing and expanding the major tradition of building. At its best the *sukiya* style softened and made more flexible the scheme of effects considered proper to serious architecture. The Katsura mansion, for example, illustrates an enhancement, in almost every instance, of *Shoin-zukuri* forms. Complementing this general development at Katsura is the bold decorativeness of the tea pavilions, so large that they can not be considered pure examples of the tea attitude. The main room of the Shokintei is placed so that the wallpaper at the back can be seen from inside the mansion, across the lake. The wallpaper can be picked out of the natural colors of earth walls, thatch roof, and foliage because its checkerboard of large squares is colored white and cerulean blue, and it flickers brightly through the green and brown landscape.

The *sukiya* style, or attitude, could also be made to yield new spatial effects without altogether sacrificing clarity of structure. One architect who achieved this balance was Enshu Kobori, the governor of Enshu province. Soldier, scholar, official, architect, and tea master, Enshu is supposed to have agreed to design a building or a garden only if three

SHOKINTEI, KATSURA IMPERIAL VILLA

From the main room there is an excellent view of an island and, in the foreground, a stone lantern to light the boat landing. *Shoji* in the upper part of the wall are protected by a bamboo lattice.

SHOIKEN, KATSURA IMPERIAL VILLA

The Shoiken is the largest tea house in Katsura's gardens. Like the Shokintei, it has stepping stones leading from the edge of the lake for those who arrive by boat. A long window is set at floor level (above) and round windows are spaced above the *shoji* (right).

SHOKINTEI, KATSURA IMPERIAL VILLA

Widely imitated, this elevation of the Shokintei's tea room is perhaps the apotheosis of picturesque architecture in Japan. Structural validity has been subordinated to effects of line and texture; the wall is an abstract composition of plaster, bamboo, paper, and wood. At the left are shelves on which feudal tea devotees placed their swords. The board door at the right shields the "crawling-in entrance." This section of the wall is approximately nine feet long.

conditions were met: no limit to the budget, no limit to time, and no interference from the client. Though it is probably of nineteenth century origin this story does sum up the high regard with which Enshu was traditionally held. He is believed, but again without adequate documentation, to have designed Katsura, its gardens, and, more likely, much of Ieyasu's mansion and all of its gardens. When he retired to Daitokuji Temple, Enshu built a large tea room called Bosen. Contrary to established practice he oriented the room toward the west. The ceiling is unusually high and the mats are arranged formally. *Shoin-zukuri* features like the *nageshi* are retained, but the *tenjo-nageshi* (the horizontal brace just under the ceiling) is omitted. The room opens, on the west, to a narrow veranda protected by an overhanging roof. Two sets of *shoji* are used, but only the innermost set closes the room to the weather. The outer set, a few inches beyond the veranda, appears suspended from the roof. It serves as a visual barrier only, stopping about six feet above the ground. Seen from inside the room this glowing panel of white light acts as a proscenium for the garden, in which trees and stone ornaments acquire a compelling dramatic interest.

It is believed that prior to its restoration in the eighteenth century the ceiling of Enshu's tea room was of white plaster, rather than boards, and the intersection of white walls, ceiling, and *shoji* without benefit of an exposed structural member must have made the room even more weightless and austere than it is now. Enshu placed his hearth near the *tokonoma,* so that he could sit facing the garden, and he delighted most in his handiwork when, in winter, with the inner *shoji* completely removed, he could drink tea while watching the snow fall mysteriously from behind his curtain of white light.

BOSEN TEA ROOM, DAITOKUJI TEMPLE

Designed by Enshu Kobori in 1636, the room preserves the structural clarity of *Shoin-zukuri* architecture while introducing new effects of scale and space. Mats are arranged to suggest a functional division of areas, the back of the room being treated as a large alcove containing the *tokonoma*.

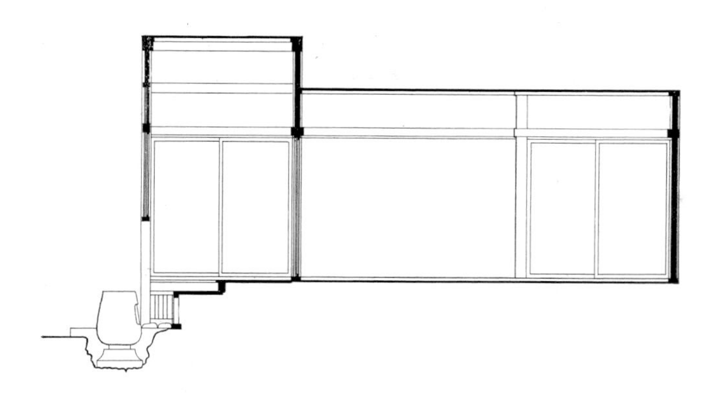

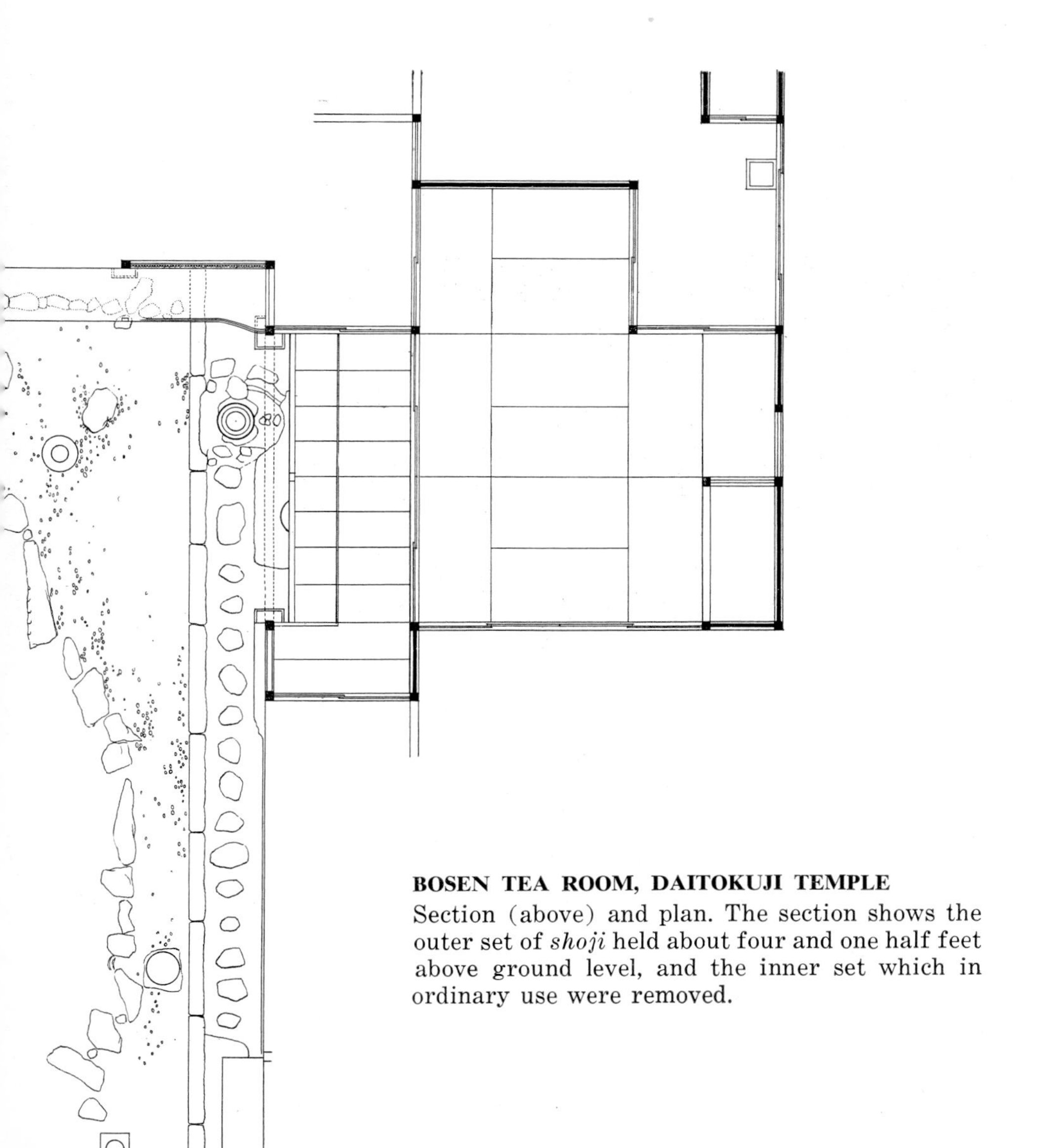

BOSEN TEA ROOM, DAITOKUJI TEMPLE

Section (above) and plan. The section shows the outer set of *shoji* held about four and one half feet above ground level, and the inner set which in ordinary use were removed.

BOSEN TEA ROOM, DAITOKUJI TEMPLE

BARN AND FARMHOUSE, KYOTO

Folk architecture makes extensive use of fixed, solid walls of plaster and wood. The roof of the barn (left) is built up of five to ten inches of earth on boards, then covered with tile.

WAREHOUSE, KYOTO

Walls are made in two sections, the inner shell of cypress planks being separated by an air space from the outer shell of plaster. A board fence protects the lower part of the wall. For protection against fire the roof is also of plaster, shielded from rain by the tile canopy which appears to float above the building. Windows visible in the background have wood shutters fireproofed with plaster.

OVERLEAF

GARDEN FENCES

Left, top: vertical bamboo poles and filling of bamboo branches; bottom: horizontal bamboo poles with branches left untrimmed. Right, top: bamboo poles in *hinoki* frames; bottom: woven split bamboo.

FIREPROOF WALL

The lower part of the wall is surfaced with gray floor tiles set diagonally. Joints are covered with plaster mouldings. The decoration of surfaces in Japanese architecture generally depends on the repetition of a simple linear pattern, rather than on sculptural effects of mass or light and shadow.

STORE, KYOTO

The store facade is made of removable panels all set on one track, with a sliding door incorporated in the center panel. The upper part of the wall may be left open or equipped with *shoji*. In warm weather all panels may be stored in a closet. The removable fence is designed to protect the wall from animals. Living quarters for the family may be at the rear, separated from the store by a small garden.

PROJECTING WINDOW

Lattice windows afford a view from within but are difficult to see into from the street. *Shoji* are not used directly behind the lattice, but are set back on the wall plane.

PROJECTING WINDOW

Facades of houses or stores on a village street may incorporate projecting lattice windows, sometimes lacquered red. The windows of this building are comparable to the one shown on the left.

PLASTER WALL

The strips of wood are decorative, but by their number may once have signified rank. Hemp fibres nailed to the strips (or to a wood framework if the wall is hollow) provide a bonding agent for several layers of earth and plaster.

The increase in urban population and the prosperity of the merchant class was due not to some planned effort on the part of the Tokugawa Shoguns, but came about despite their efforts to limit such developments. The military vassals of the Shogunate and their *samurai* found themselves borrowing from the merchants in order to buy and maintain the accoutrements appropriate to their class; farmers, no longer able to barter with rice, required more and more money, and so the wealth of the country shifted from the military aristocracy to the new urban middle classes. Speculation in rice or a bad crop sometimes produced the misery requisite to peasant rebellions, while those who understood the advantages of foreign trade chafed under restrictions which kept the country closed to the rest of the world. In 1868, when pressures from within and without could no longer be resisted, the monarchy was restored to power and Japan was opened to the West.

Contact with other nations brought problems unprecedented in Japan and often unsolved by the West itself. Foremost among these were, and still are, problems of industrialization. In their haste to adapt at least the obvious features of European and American civilizations, Japanese architects encountered difficulties in some ways similar to those encountered in England and the United States, where many new activities were being housed in buildings not originally intended for them. The Japanese first absorbed Western architecture primarily as a building technique. Architects trained abroad could cope with many of the problems they were called upon to solve, but for major buildings the services of foreign architects were deemed appropriate. In this respect the Japanese were merely continuing a tradition already active when monk-architects were imported from Korea or China, to design such major works as Horyuji Temple or the Daibutsuden of Todaiji Temple. Thus the battlemented Historical Museum and The Italian Renaissance General Staff Office in Tokyo were designed by the Italian C. V. Capeletti, in 1881. Josiah Condor of England built a Russian Orthodox Church in 1891, and R. P. Bridgens from America, de Boinville from France, and Herman Ende from Germany, among others, contributed government buildings, universities, banks, museums, arsenals, and railway stations in styles as varied as were their architects' nationalities. Unlike previous importations from China and Korea, these exotic works brought with them quite new ways of living. For esthetic reasons their individual "styles" would have been open to question even in their countries of origin. In Japan they produced much confusion.

In 1910 the Architectural Institute of Japan made the

problem the subject of a symposium. Two major objections to Western styles were expressed at that time. First, all of the styles were too far removed from Japanese taste. Second, the Japanese, traditionally accustomed to sacrificing comfort in order to live in close contact with their natural surroundings, found that thick stone walls and small windows were ill adapted to their climate. Inadequate ventilating and heating facilities made some of the Western style buildings almost impossible to use. However, the industrialization of the country and the continuing absorption of Western ideas required new building types for which Japanese architecture offered no models. The conclusion was that the use of Western architectural "styles" would of necessity be continued, but that their evils should be mitigated by the introduction of Japanese features. Since the beliefs that had produced those features were themselves being questioned, it proved increasingly difficult to graft superficial Japanese details onto Western concepts, in architecture as in everything else.

After World War I the need for a new architecture was literally brought home to the public: a style of living considered modern found increasing favor for home life, and many private homes were designed in European styles. While the exteriors of such houses suggested English or Dutch villas, the number of Western style rooms they actually contained depended on financial resources and on the amount of discomfort the family was prepared to endure. At the back of the house there was likely to be a Japanese garden and clean, airy rooms of traditional Japanese design, ostensibly for less adaptable parents and grandparents but often a refuge for the whole family. In most cases a man in a Western business suit, returning from a day at the office, donned a kimono the moment he entered his English cottage. His office probably had central heating, which made a light business suit appropriate, but central heating or gas heaters set in fireplaces may have been too costly for home use, thus making a warm, quilted kimono desirable.

Some outstanding contributions to the development of modern Japanese architecture were made by foreigners who came to live and work in Japan. Some of them were well acquainted with European and American efforts to devise a new architecture, and they recognized in the traditional architecture of Japan principles of obvious relevance to the West. At that moment in Japan, however, it was just those traditional habits of building that were deemed irrelevant, or, more precisely, they seemed the property of conservative elements of the community interested in impeding rather than advancing the creative capacities of Japan's younger architects. The German architect Bruno Taut lived for a time

IMPERIAL HOTEL, TOKYO

Frank Lloyd Wright, architect. 1916-1922.

Brick walls are ornamented with carved lava stone. Pools surrounding the building maintain a water supply during severe earthquakes.

in Japan, admired its architectural heritage, and through his writing diverted attention from such flamboyant works as Nikko to the classic purity of the Katsura Palace. Taut's enthusiasm helped re-establish in Japan an attitude towards building which the Western world was only then developing for itself.

Antonin Raymond opened his own office in Japan in 1921. His work has often pioneered technical and esthetic solutions of great value to Japanese architects, many of whom completed their training in his office. Of Raymond's more recent buildings an apartment house built in 1951 for staff members of the United States Department of State is a characteristic example of his ability to utilize Japanese craftsmanship in new ways. The smooth walls of the apartment house are of concrete without any additional surfacing material, and the building depends for its effect largely on the precision with which the wood formwork was made.

Frank Lloyd Wright's Imperial Hotel, built in Tokyo in 1918-22, rests on caissons floating in the mud fields Ieyasu reclaimed for his vassals. The heavy massing of this building, the undistinguished color of its brick walls, and the coarsely ornamented lava stone used throughout combine to make the exterior an excessively personal statement. But some of the interiors are prodigies of architectural space, at that time new not only to Japan but to the rest of the world. Particularly is this so of the entrance lobby and the main dining room, where changing ceiling heights and floor levels allow natural light to be used with great dramatic effect.

While they found much to admire in Wright's work it is not surprising that most Japanese architects did not directly benefit from it, nor have they since 1922. Examples pertinent to their problems were found instead in the work of Walter Gropius and the Bauhaus, Le Corbusier, and Mies van der Rohe. Many architects went abroad to study and work with these men, and the most successful attempts to create a new architecture conformed in varying degrees with the ideas and practices of European functionalism, although Le Corbusier and Mies van der Rohe are not properly identified with that doctrine. Early in the 1920s a group of Japanese architects, believing that all "styles" are harmful, and that good architecture is the automatic result of good planning and the honest expression of function, produced a series of buildings that seemed allied with traditional values despite the novelty of their appearance. *Art Nouveau,* and particularly the Vienna *Sezession,* seemed to correspond to the Japanese feeling for nature in its enthusiasm for motifs drawn from plant forms, and so they called themselves the Secessionists. Among them was Sutemi Horiguchi, an architect whose com-

APARTMENT HOUSE, TOKYO
Raymond and Rado, architects. 1952.
Built for staff members of the United States Department of State, this concrete apartment house incorporates cantilevered balconies and sliding glass walls.

OKADA HOUSE AND GARDENS, TOKYO
Sutemi Horiguchi, architect. 1933.

The wall, the garden, and the rectangular pool are sharply defined horizontal planes decorated by stones and plants of widely contrasting textures. The bamboo terrace recalls the Moon Viewing Platform of the Katsura Imperial Villa.

WAKASA HOUSE, TOKYO
Sutemi Horiguchi, architect. 1939.
The house is composed of interpenetrating volumes related to the garden by a ramp and a long rectangular pool.

prehension of the undeclared, even disclaimed, formal esthetic motives underlying modern Western architecture was remarkably complete. Horiguchi's Wakasa house, built in 1939, recalls the work of Walter Gropius in its asymmetric, cubic massing and structurally unarticulated stucco surfaces, but a long, narrow swimming pool at right angles to the house introduces a landscape-building relationship peculiarly Japanese.

Under the aegis of a militant nationalism the mixing of styles was revived, in the 1930s, with a new emphasis on forms of Oriental origin. To Western eyes perhaps the most unnerving product of this effort is the Honganji Temple in Tokyo, built in 1934. The interior of this concrete Buddhist temple is primarily Japanese, while its stone exterior combines Indian stupas and a barrel vault with an Italian Renaissance stair and a basement carrying a single giant order of Indian columns, between which are wide windows recalling German Classicism. Once regarded as a model for further development, this style has not gained wide acceptance.

Skeleton structures of steel or concrete, sheathed with blank stucco surfaces, offered the purity required by Japanese taste. But the enthusiasm for an architecture seemingly without "style" led to buildings which looked, in the words Frank Lloyd Wright has applied to their European counterparts, cut out of cardboard rather than constructed of solid materials. The preferred corrective for this has been derived largely from the work of Le Corbusier. An example is the Nippon Sogo Bank by Kunio Maekawa, an architect who worked with Le Corbusier in the 1930s. On the first three storeys the round columns of the Bank are exposed, not as free-standing *pilotis* but as engaged columns. For the remaining storeys the cantilevered facade conceals the columns and is divided, on the upper floors, into a pattern of glazed and solid surfaces articulated by projecting balconies and by slight recessions in the wall plane.

A somewhat different esthetic underlies the work of Junzo Sakakura, who also worked with Le Corbusier. Sakakura designed the Japanese Pavilion at the 1937 Paris Exposition, and in that building he employed the open structural cage, the modular regularity, and the delicate scale of traditional Japanese architecture with a precision and clarity hardly surpassed in Japan since then. Sakakura's Museum of Modern Art building in Kamakura, near Tokyo, retains some of this direct handling of varied elements, but is perhaps most interesting for its use of details characteristic of *Sukiya-zukuri* architecture, however unrelated to tea house design they may at first appear to be. Steel columns, for example, seem to rest on stones floating in a pond at one side of the

NIPPON SOGO BANK, TOKYO
Kunio Maekawa, architect. 1952.
Exterior walls are of glass and prefabricated concrete slabs. Exposed columns, projecting balconies, and the placement of windows on the upper floors are designed to add sculptural interest.

JAPANESE PAVILION, PARIS
Junzo Sakakura, architect. 1937.
A temporary building in the Paris Exposition of 1937, Sakakura's pavilion was a light steel cage filled with walls of glass or wood.

MUSEUM OF MODERN ART, KAMAKURA
Junzo Sakakura, architect. 1951.
The exhibition floor containing skylighted galleries is raised above ground on thin steel columns and encloses an open court. Walls at ground level are masonry; other walls are of asbestos panels with aluminum joints.

MUSEUM OF MODERN ART, KAMAKURA
Junzo Sakakura, architect. 1951.
The gallery floor is carried out over a pond. Foundation stones in the water are actually decorative accessories attached to the columns.

building. The galleries are carried one floor above ground by these columns, and so the building projects over the water. But the columns do not in fact rest on the stones: instead they extend well beneath the floor of the pond, where they are tied to each other by concrete foundation walls. The stones are expressive symbols of support, and the craftsmanship with which they have been cut through to accommodate the columns rivals the meticulousness of traditional carpentry. Again, a steel column lands directly in the center of the main stair, presumably to emphasize the regularity of the structural system, but it will also recall tea house windows bisected by bamboo columns or braces.

Few Japanese architects have pursued this adaptation of poetically inspired details. Sculpturally modeled form has seemed more important. The imposition of a plastic form on a linear structural skeleton produces difficulties for Japanese and Western architects alike. There is, however, this difference: the plasticity so much admired in the work of Le Corbusier has behind it centuries of Mediterranean tradition. In Japan there is no equivalent sustaining tradition of sculptural form; on the contrary, except in the design of roofs Japanese architecture has in the past been essentially planar and linear. The concern with sculptural qualities also leads to "style," and a concern with style is equated by some Japanese critics with a reprehensible indifference to what the United States has already experienced as "social realism." It is true that this point of view has been most compelling to those who are primarily interested in social and political reform.

The architecture of Ludwig Mies van der Rohe has had relatively little influence in Japan. One reason for this would appear to be the need, both for safety and economy, of earthquake-proof reinforced concrete structures. Mies' architecture has been centered largely on the problems of designing with steel, and his buildings have seemed to offer no immediately applicable lessons. Indeed, much that Western architects admire in Mies' work is perhaps overlooked by the Japanese for no other reason than its resemblance, perhaps superficial, to a tradition which is itself ignored. Attempts to revive that tradition have met with difficulties. Sutemi Horiguchi, in his recent work, has abandoned many of his earlier ideas and has developed *Shoin-zukuri* and *Sukiya-zukuri* forms with skill and imagination. But such exclusively traditional statements are possible now only through small buildings. Antonin Raymond, in his residential work, has attempted to rationalize traditional systems of construction. Other architects, and decorators, have adapted superficial details to make modernized versions of traditional buildings, similar to American "modernizations" of colonial archi-

FACULTY CLUB ROOM, KEIO UNIVERSITY, TOKYO
Isamu Noguchi, designer. 1952.

The faculty club room at Keio University was designed by the American sculptor Isamu Noguchi in memory of his father, a professor at the University for many years. The background for the hearth and the sitting area around it is a white *tokonoma* and a wall of red tile. Two concrete columns, one structural, the other serving as a flue, support a curved metal hood for the fireplace. The designer has given a new solidity to the Japanese interior by adding new elements and modifying old ones.

tecture except for a curious chic that renders them boneless.

A noteworthy example of the adaptation of traditional forms is a group of buildings designed by Kenzo Tange for the Hiroshima Memorial Peace Center. This project consists of two buildings and an arch. The larger of the buildings is a museum raised above ground on *pilotis*. The facades are equipped with vertical louvres for protection against the sun. Nearby is a building to house a library, offices, and conference rooms. Where the museum depends for its effect on sculpturally rounded forms, including facades almost imperceptibly concave, the library building is an enlarged version in concrete of the traditional wood cage. Its proportions recall the upper and lower wall panels of a traditional Japanese house. The powerful forms of cantilevered stairs in the museum building suggest the steps and galleries of the Imperial Palace in Kyoto.

It would appear that modern architecture in Japan must first be international—that is to say, visually and structurally related to twentieth century technology—before it can become specifically Japanese. In Japan more than in other countries the tradition of pre-industrial building offers much that the modern architect finds sympathetic and useful. To maintain continuity with the past would seem, to the Western architect, easier for his Japanese colleague than for himself. But hidden in the Japanese tradition is a strong preference, as Bruno Taut observed, for irrational structure. Confronted with Western technology this drive has only infrequently succeeded in transforming Western techniques: more often it is itself reduced to arbitrary stylishness. An example of the interaction of Japanese and Western assumptions is Kenzo Tange's exhibition building for the Kobe Trade Fair, built in 1950. The building is a wood cage, but steel bolts and plates replace traditional carpenter's details. In a further effort to rationalize the structure the architect has chosen to use diagonal bracing. Behind the braces are light wood and glass panels, related in scale to *shoji*. The exposed bracing is perhaps more forthright than most Western architects—probably influenced by traditional Japanese standards—would allow, but the peculiar effectiveness of this building owes much to its architect's grasp of what is vital both in the developing architecture of the West and in his own tradition.

To a Western observer Japan seems to have been populated entirely by gifted architects. The national talent for making buildings has not diminished, but the problems with which architects contend have increased.

ARITOMI HOUSE, TOKYO
Junzo Yoshimura, architect. 1953.
Columns are of cryptomeria with only the top bark removed. Walls are screens of glass which slide into storage closets, thus enabling the house to be completely opened in a few minutes. The closets are an adaptation of the traditional *amado* in which *shoji* are stored.

MASUZAWA HOUSE, TOKYO
Makato Masuzawa, architect. 1952.

The house is approximately eighteen feet wide. It preserves aspects of traditional Japanese design while incorporating elements of Western planning; the interior is one large room two storeys high, with a balcony at the rear.

MEMORIAL PEACE CENTER, HIROSHIMA

Kenzo Tange, architect. Begun 1951.

The center occupies a thirty acre site and will contain conference halls, a museum, and other facilities for international use in the promotion of peace. The buildings were photographed in the course of construction.

Library building. Model.

EXHIBITION BUILDING, KOBE
Kenzo Tange, architect. 1950.

Intricate carpentry joints were replaced by a system of bolts and steel plates, and prefabricated panels of wood and glass replaced *shoji*. The lightness of the structure is made possible by diagonal bracing, boldly expressed on the facades.

4

SUPPLEMENT: JAPANESE EXHIBITION HOUSE

The Museum's Japanese Exhibition House was made in Nagoya in 1953. Together with all accessories it was shipped to the United States in 700 crates. Among the items included were prefabricated panels of *hinoki* (cypress) bark shingles for the roof, lanterns, fences, furnishings, and kitchen utensils, stones of all sizes and coarse white sand for the gardens. The entire building was reassembled in the Museum's garden under the supervision of the architect, Junzo Yoshimura, with the assistance of four craftsmen trained for this project in Japan by Heizaemon Ito, who was chief carpenter. The garden was designed by the architect and Tansai Sano; the latter directed its assembly in New York.

A Japanese building was chosen by the Museum for its third *House in the Garden* because traditional Japanese design has a unique relevance to modern Western architecture. The characteristics which give it this relevance are post and lintel skeleton frame construction; flexibility of plan; close relation of indoor and outdoor areas; and the decorative use of structural elements.

Japanese architecture is known in the United States largely through exhibition buildings such as those seen at the Chicago Columbian Exposition of 1893, the New York and San Francisco World's Fairs of 1939, and through published examples of tea houses, farm buildings, and folk architecture in general. Visitors returning from Japan are often familiar with urban homes of semi-traditional design, but have not always been able to see the great monuments of Japanese architecture.

The Museum's Exhibition House was chosen to illustrate some of the characteristics of buildings considered by the Japanese to be masterpieces, and considered by Western architects to be of continuing relevance to our own building activities. These requirements called for a more disciplined esthetic and a wider technical range than is found in tea houses or farm buildings, however beautiful they may be. The kind of building that seemed to fulfill the requirements most satisfactorily was the residential complex of the sixteenth and seventeenth centuries, developed for the aristocracy and particularly for the military retainers called *samurai* under circumstances explained elsewhere in this book. Surviving examples from this period are most often found adjoining temples, where they served as residences for priests. Because the main room of such a house is equipped with a desk called *shoin,* the building type was designated *Shoin-zukuri,* which means the *shoin* way of building.

Limitations of the site and problems attendant on making the house accessible to the public imposed the following adjustments:

1. Orientation. The main rooms of the house would ordinarily have faced southeast. Adjoining buildings predetermined an orientation to the west, overlooking the Museum's sculpture garden.

2. Number and size of rooms. Houses of this design consisted of one, two, or three units, essentially similar and arranged asymmetrically. Rooms did not differ greatly and were interchangeable. The Exhibition House presents one basic unit. The *ken* module used throughout the main building is approximately 6½ feet, measured from the center of one column to the center of the next. Storage rooms (number 13 on the plan) were reduced in size. The veranda north of the *shoin* room (number 8 on the plan) was made somewhat larger than usual to facilitate the movement of large crowds. A complete tea house, a kitchen, and a bathroom appropriate to the period were included, but servants' quarters were omitted. No attempt was made to artificially age the wood by darkening it. The house presents intact a phase of Japanese architecture as it originally appeared.

JAPANESE EXHIBITION HOUSE

The Museum of Modern Art, New York. 1954, 1955.

Presented by the America-Japan Society, Tokyo, on behalf of the people of Japan, and sponsored by private citizens in Japan and the United States, and the Museum of Modern Art, New York.

Junzo Yoshimura	Architect
Heizaemon Ito	Chief Carpenter
Tansai Sano	Gardener
Arthur Drexler	Director
Philip C. Johnson	Consultant
George M. Hopkinson	Consultant
Natalie Hoyt	Coordinator
Edward Winter	Construction Supervisor
Ethelbert Furlong	Garden Consultant

SPECIAL COMMITTEE OF THE AMERICA-JAPAN SOCIETY, TOKYO.

Architectural Advisors: Kunio Maekawa, Junzo Sakakura, Junzo Yoshimura, Chisaburoh Yamada, Soyetsu Yanagi. *Advisors:* Yazo Anzo, Kojiro Abe, Konosuke Akiyama, Shinsuke Asao, Ryozo Asano, Ichiro Ishikawa, Taizo Ishisaka, Shojiro Ishibashi, Hisato Ichimada, Eiichiro Iwase, Aisuke Kabayama, Teiichi Kawakita, Konosuke Koike, Ataru Kobayashi, Masakazu Kobayashi, Takashi Komatsu, Kiyoshi Goko, Yaichi Sasaki, Kiichiro Sato, Kyonosuke Sakai, Seiji Sako, Keizo Shibusawa, Yasuo Shimizu, Michisuke Sugi, Keizo Seki, Seiichiro Takahashi, Tokujiro Tanaka, Kyosuke Tamai, Sozaburo Chigira, Kiyoshi Togasaki, Motoichi Toyama, Risaburo Torigai, Mototada Nakamura, Masakazu Nagata, Shigeo Nagano, Katsuhiko Hamaguchi, Aiichiro Fujiyama, Josaku Furusawa, Takeyoshi Hari, Shozo Hotta, Chikao Honda, Yoshiichi Murakami, Ichiro Yano, Tamesaburo Yamamoto, Tadao Watanabe, Gisuke Watanabe.

The Museum wishes to thank, in addition to the members of the Special Committee, the following individuals for their advice and assistance: Antonin Raymond, Mr. and Mrs. Yoneo Arai, Isamu Noguchi, Douglas Overton, Alan Priest, R. C. Kramer.

1 GARDEN ENTRANCE
2 FAMILY ENTRANCE
3 GALLERY
4 SECOND ROOM
5 FIRST ROOM
   a – *shoin* (desk)
   b – *chigai-dana* (shelves)
   c – *tokonoma* (alcove)
6 VERANDA
   a – *chumon* (vestibule for garden entrance)
   b – *nure-en* (outer or "wet" veranda)
7 GARDEN
8 SIDE VERANDA
9 BRIDGE (to tea house and bath)
10 TEA HOUSE PANTRY
11 TEA CEREMONY ROOM
12 BATH
   a – main room
   b – toilet
13 STORAGE ROOM
14 GALLERY
15 SERVICE VERANDA
16 PANTRY
17 KITCHEN
   a – stove

Drawing by Dale Byrd

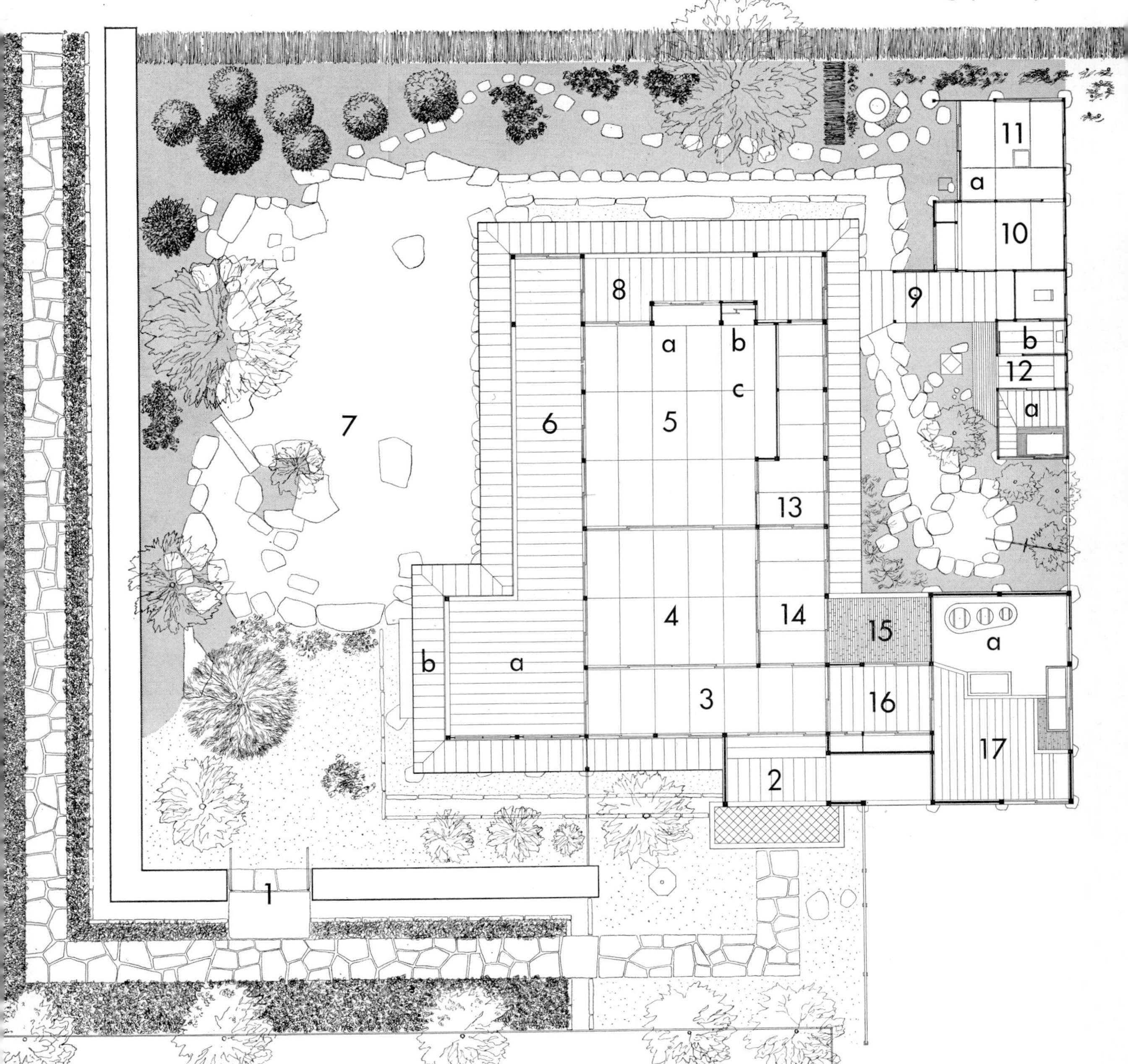

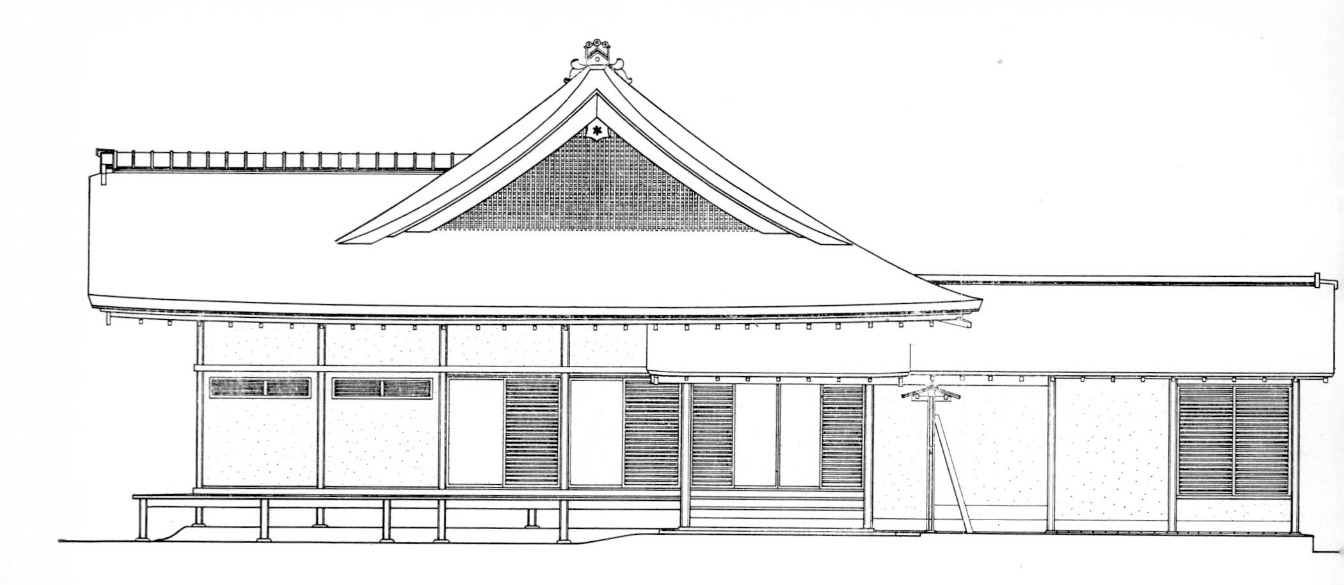

South elevation.

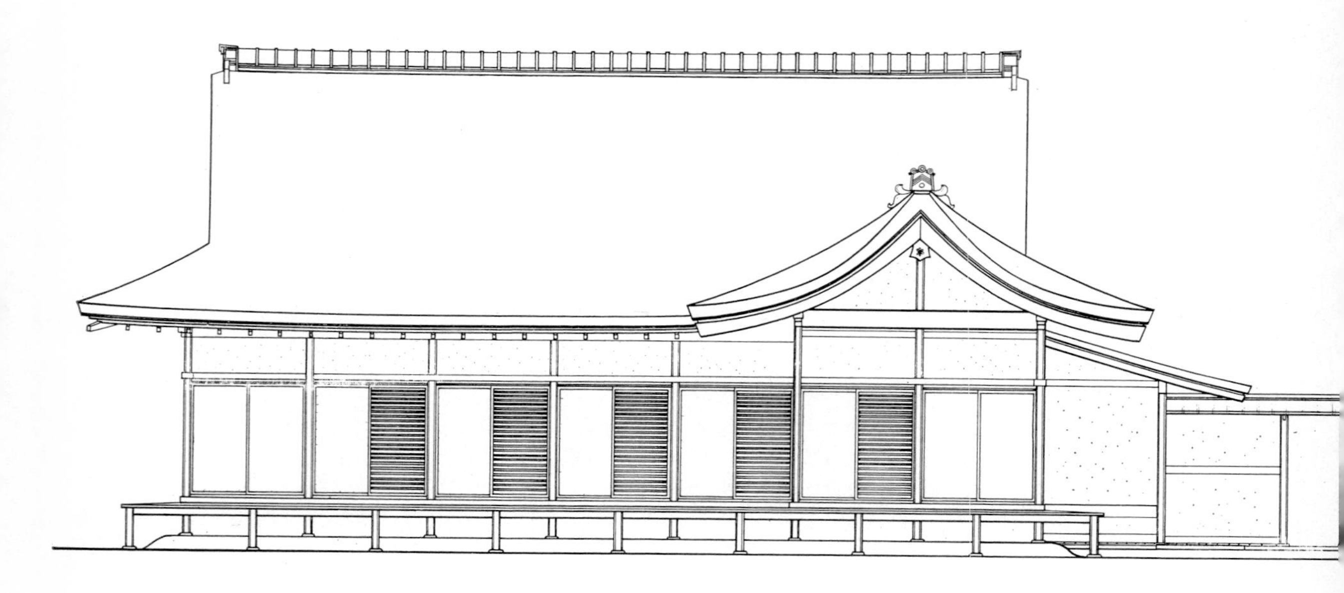

West elevation.

SCALE: 6½ foot *ken* module, measured from column centers.

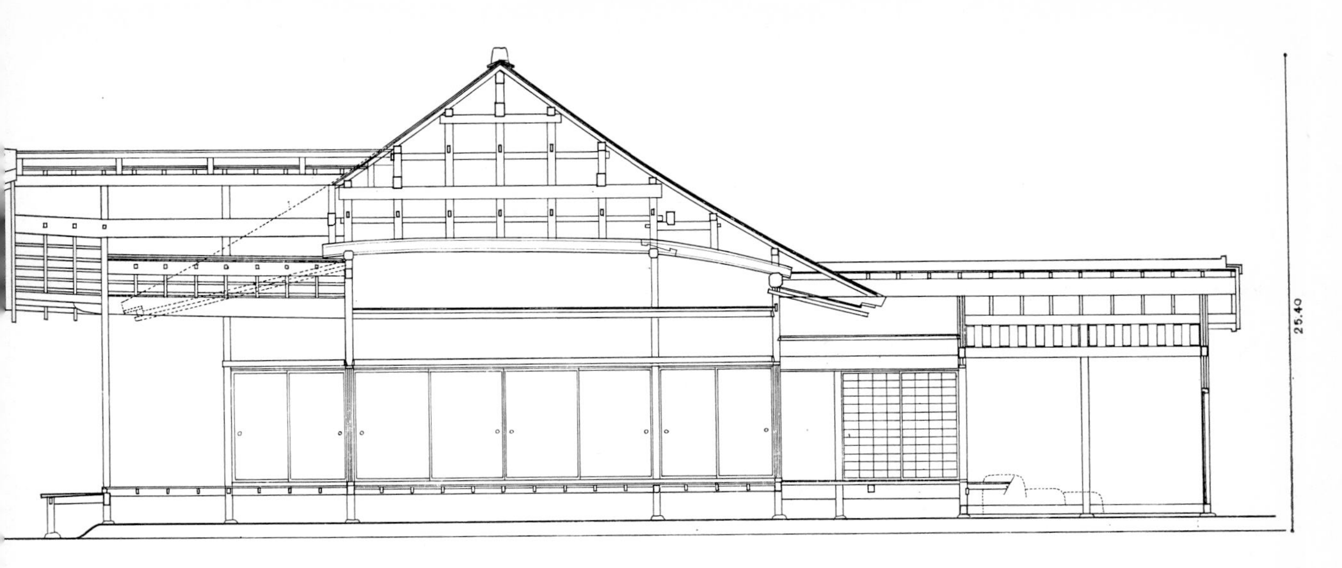

Section looking north.

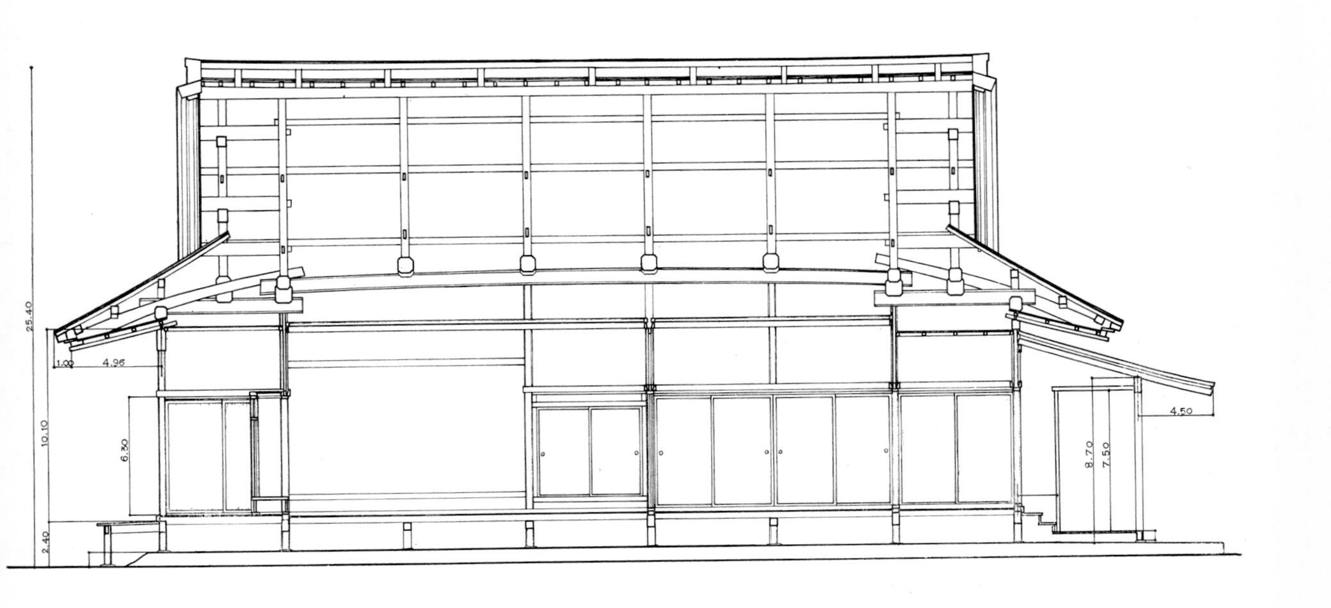

Section looking east.

JAPANESE EXHIBITION HOUSE
Museum of Modern Art.

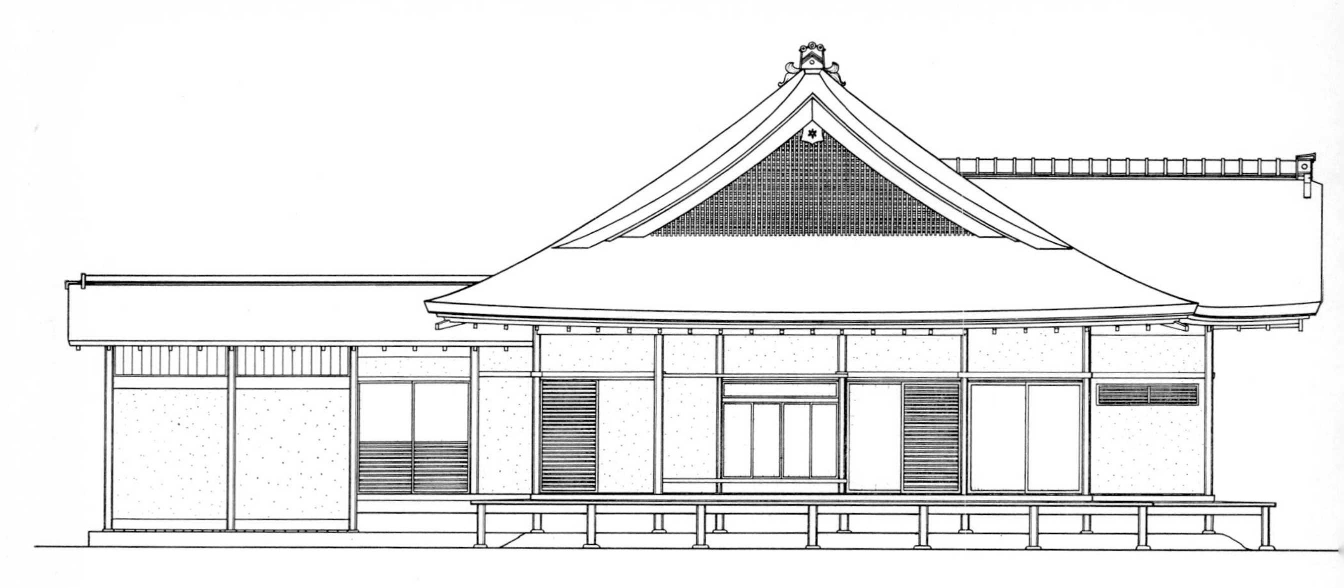

East elevation.

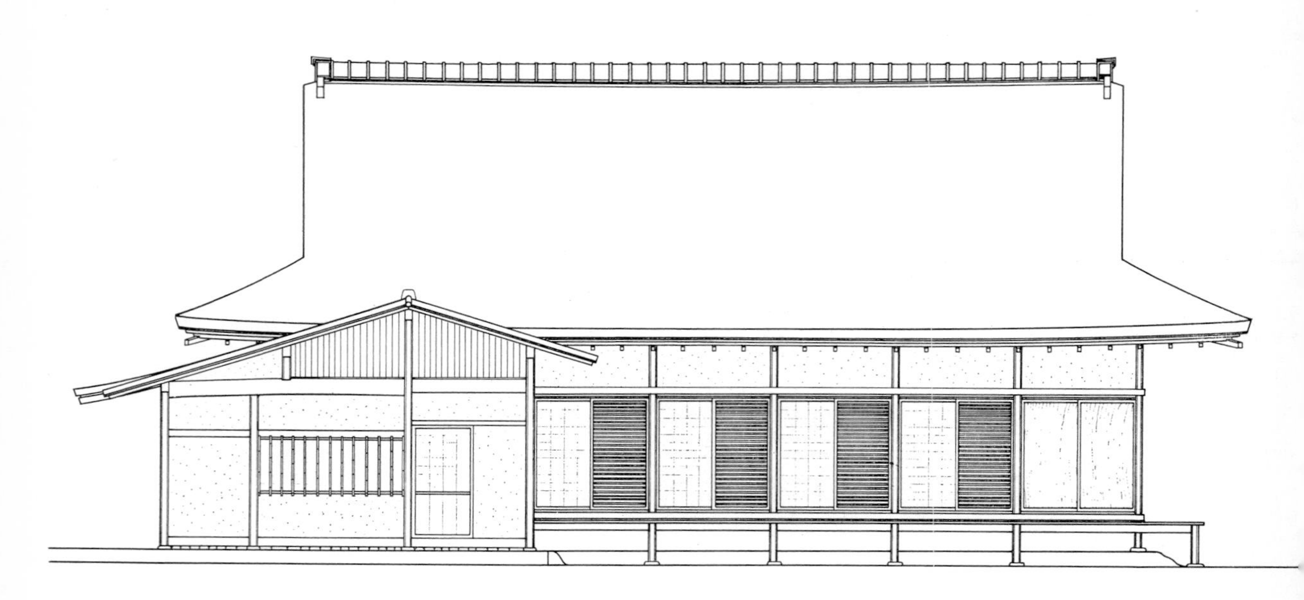

North elevation.

JAPANESE EXHIBITION HOUSE
Museum of Modern Art.

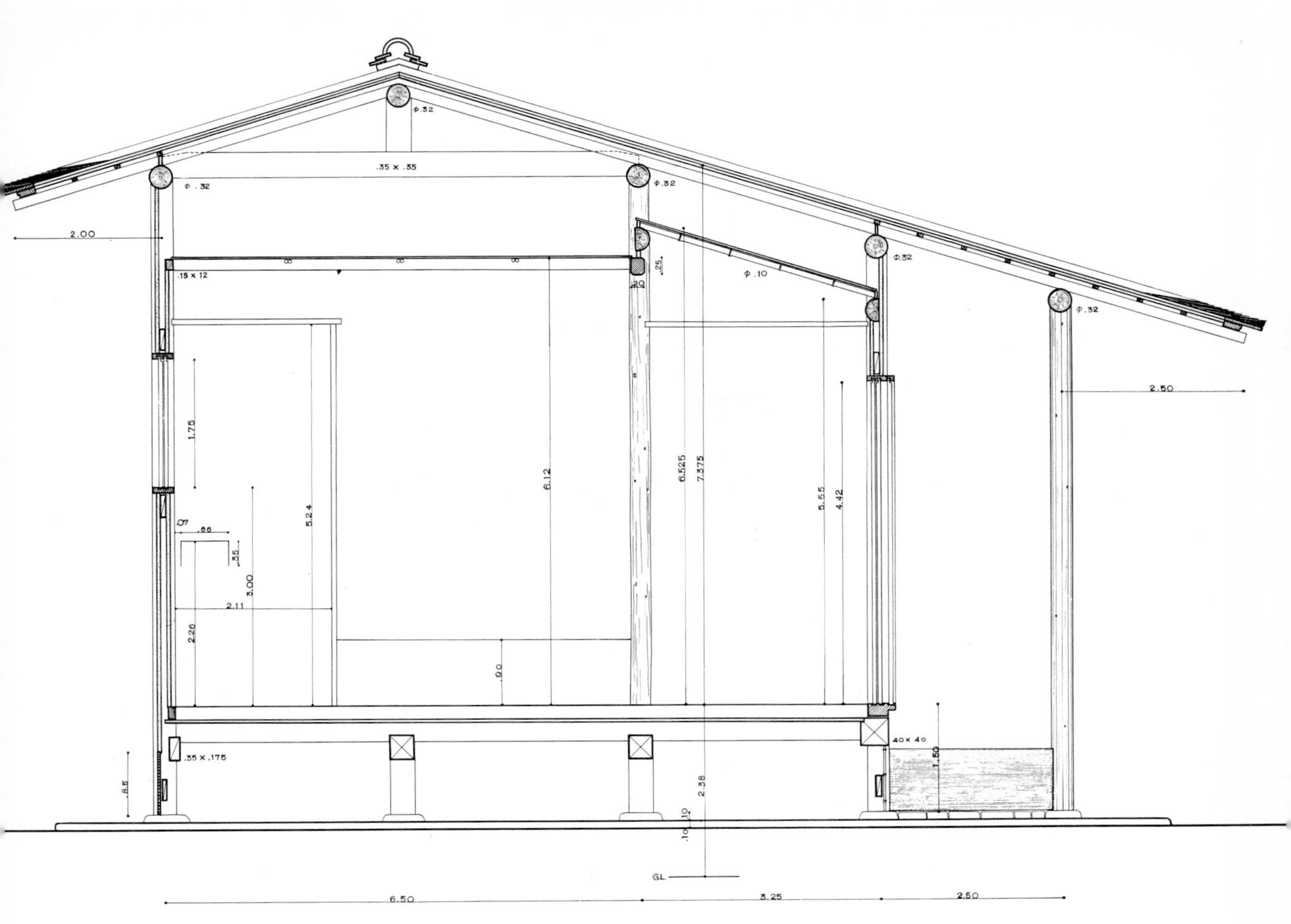

Section looking south.

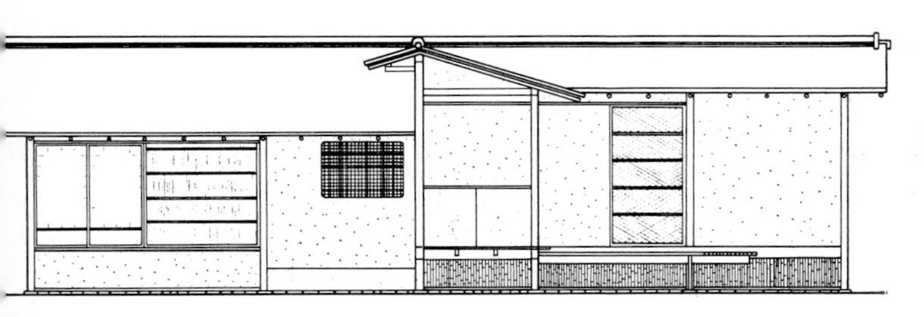

South elevation.

TEA HOUSE

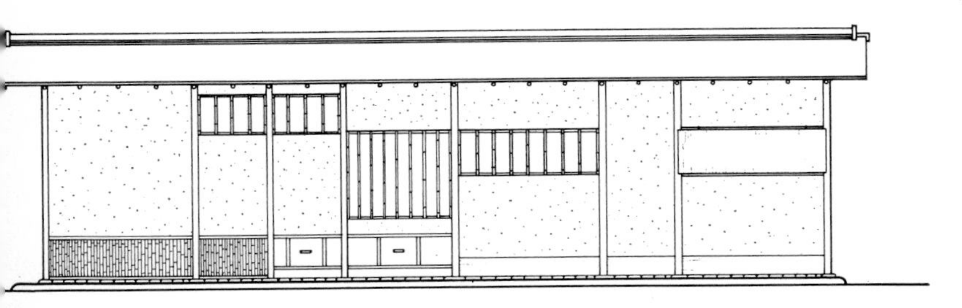

North elevation.

Garden entrance.

JAPANESE EXHIBITION HOUSE
Museum of Modern Art.

Pool and veranda.

Pool and veranda.

Lantern outside the entrance gallery.

JAPANESE EXHIBITION HOUSE
Museum of Modern Art.

First and second rooms with exterior walls removed for summer use.

Family entrance.

First and second rooms. The mats are bound with patterned silk tape.

Pool seen from the veranda adjoining the second room.

JAPANESE EXHIBITION HOUSE
Museum of Modern Art.

First (*shoin*) room with landscape paintings in black ink.

The *shoin* (desk) in the background is adjoined by storage shelves. The *tokonoma* is at the right.

Main garden.

Waterfall in the main garden.

Veranda. Rafters are hung from beams inside the roof and serve primarily for decoration.

Tea house. Walls are of ochre-colored Kyoto earth.

JAPANESE EXHIBITION HOUSE
Museum of Modern Art.

JAPANESE EXHIBITION HOUSE
Museum of Modern Art.

Rear garden. The small veranda leads to the bathroom.

Bridge to tea house and bath.

Bamboo service veranda.

Kitchen. The oven, at ground level, is made of earth and waxed plaster. A charcoal fire is kept in the sandbox (foreground). Drainboard and sink are at the rear.

Kitchen work space adjoins a pantry, where portable tables are stored in cabinets and food is prepared for serving on shelf just above floor level.

Bathroom. Sunken wood tub adjoins sliding lattice screen and waxed *shoji*. The roof is of *hinoki* bark shingles.

JAPANESE EXHIBITION HOUSE
Museum of Modern Art.

The roof is of *hinoki* bark shingles.

PHOTOGRAPH CREDITS

Page 12, Germaine Kellerman; 13, courtesy Jiro Harada; 21, Harada; 24, 25, Francis Haar; 26, 29, 30, 33, courtesy Ise Shrine; 34, Haar; 36, 37, 38, courtesy Ise Shrine; 40, 42, 50, Yasuhiro Ishimoto; 51, Tansai Sano; 52, Arthur Drexler; 53, 54, 64, Ishimoto; 70, Drexler; 72, 76, 79, Tatsuzo Sato; 80, courtesy Yakushiji Temple; 81, 84, 85, Sato; 86, Drexler; 87, 89, 90, 91, Sato; 92, Ishimoto; 94, 95, courtesy Alexander C. Soper; 100, 102, 103, 104, 105, 106, 108, 109, 110, Sato; 112, Kellerman; 116, 118, 119, Sato; 124, Kellerman; 128, 131, Sato; 132, 133, 134, 135, courtesy Nijo; 138, Drexler; 139, 141, 142, Sato; 143, Drexler; 148, 149, courtesy Sutemi Horiguchi; 150–156, Sato; 158, Ryuichi Hamaguchi; 159, Drexler; 160–169, Sato; 171, Loch Crane; 173, 175, 177, Sato; 178, Ishimoto; 181, courtesy Ryoanji Temple; 182, 183 Sato; 184, Drexler; 185, Isamu Noguchi; 187, Sato; 188, Ishimoto; 189, Noguchi; 190, 191, Ishimoto; 192–194, Sato; 195, Noguchi; 196, Sato; 197, Noguchi; 198, 199, Drexler; 201, Sato; 202, 203, Drexler; 204, Kellerman; 206, Soichi Sunami; 209, Drexler; 210, 212–215, 217, Sato; 218, 219, Hamaguchi; 220–224, 229, Sato; 230, Ishimoto; 231, Sano; 232, 233, Ishimoto; 234, Drexler; 235–237, Sano; 238, Drexler; 243, Antonin Raymond; 244–246, Yoshio Watanabe; 248, 249, Watanabe; 250–252, 254, 256, 257, Chuji Hirayama; 258, 259, Kenzo Tange, Hirayama; 260, 261, Hirayama.

Photographs of the Japanese Exhibition House are by Ezra Stoller, with the exception of page 286, by Paul Berg.

The map on page 10 is used through the courtesy of Alexander Leydenfrost.

This book was printed in April 1955 for the Trustees of the Museum of Modern Art, by the Plantin Press, New York.

Book designed by Arthur Drexler.